MW00527004

VIRGINIA
Honey

VIRGINIA Honey

·A SWEET HISTORY·

VIRGINIA C. JOHNSON

AMERICAN PALATE

Published by American Palate
A Division of The History Press
Charleston, SC
www.historypress.com

Copyright © 2021 by Virginia Johnson
All rights reserved

First published 2021

Manufactured in the United States

ISBN 9781467146890

Library of Congress Control Number: 2021938365

Notice: The information in this book is true and complete to the best of our knowledge. It is offered without guarantee on the part of the author or The History Press. The author and The History Press disclaim all liability in connection with the use of this book.

All rights reserved. No part of this book may be reproduced or transmitted in any form whatsoever without prior written permission from the publisher except in the case of brief quotations embodied in critical articles and reviews.

CONTENTS

CONTENTS

INTRODUCTION

When spring comes round, Virginia's fields, meadows and gardens are filled with flowering plants that draw the honeybees from their hives. In cold weather, they huddle together, beating their small wings to warm the air around them, keeping themselves fed from stocks of honey carefully gathered over the warmer seasons.

For tended bees, their remaining honey may have been supplemented by their beekeepers. Wild bees will not receive any help—but they usually get to keep all their honey. Types of honey vary by what the bees consume. You may be tasting the special flavors that come from wildflowers or buckwheat or clover, all harvested by the bees at different times of the year. Honeybees, domestic and wild, have been hard at work in our state for approximately four hundred years.

Arriving at Jamestown by ship in the 1620s, those first honeybees swarmed, as they will, doubling and dividing their numbers into separate colonies once or twice a season. Some were coaxed into fresh hives. Others escaped into the countryside, making it possible for adventurous souls to harvest honey in the wilderness or stock their own bees at home by chopping out the occupied sections of trees and bravely hauling them back to their farms.

Recently, there has been increased interest in honey's historical past. Numerous sites throughout the Commonwealth have discovered a sweet sideline by keeping their own bees and selling the resulting honey.

While I make no claim to be a beekeeper, I very much respect both the hobbyists and professionals I have met while researching this book. I discovered that there is much joy among beekeepers—and a wish to spread that joy, as well as their knowledge, to others. I hope to do the same here in a modest way, showing how bees have sweetened the lives of humans and how humans have striven to understand and be better caretakers for their bees.

If you are interested in being a beekeeper, there are resources in a later chapter that should give you a beeline to state and local groups that can get you on your way. If you enjoy day trips, you may find the listings of places to visit helpful. There are honey recipes inspired by times past for cooks. And, if you garden, even a small area, there are suggestions on planting for pollinators, something that can help the bees, whosoever they may be.

THE HIVE MIND

I t is good to get a grounding in the basics of how the beehive works before we go into the past—where they did not necessarily know the details, as hives can be dark and dangerous places for those perceived as predators.

First, keep in mind that bees' purpose is to reproduce successfully. This is more of a challenge than it might seem from the outset, as many the sad owner of an empty hive would tell you. To nourish their growing young and themselves, honeybees need honey. To store the honey, they need wax comb. All of this they make, and they *will* make it, whether they fashion a home in a modern hive, a skep of ancient design, the hollow of a tree or spaces under the siding of an old house. A typical active hive contains twenty to sixty thousand bees.

There are three types of bees in a hive: the workers, the queen and the drones. The workers, all female, take care of their queen, who does not leave the hive, except to mate or to swarm. The workers also feed the young, still encased in comb; keep the hive clean—and defend it from invaders; create the comb; and shore up its walls with propolis to keep it strong.

Workers also gather the nectar from whatever is flowering into their stomachs and bring it back in the hive to chew on it some more and disgorge it as honey into the comb. Unpleasant as that might sound, the workers' careful processing turns the nectar into something that is greatly beneficial to humans. Honey has been used for healing—both topically and as part of medicines to take internally—and to preserve other foods.

Bees "fanning" on the front of a beehive to maintain proper temperature inside at Fort Barnard Community Garden. *Photo by Arlington County, Virginia. CC BY-SA 2.0.*

Bees do not live very long, but some live longer than others. Bees born in the spring may live about six weeks. Others will take their place, of course, assuming there is no disease. But bees that hatch in the fall cannot be so easily replaced, as winter is a time of dormancy with no fresh brood ready to replace them. Those bees will live longer to overwinter with the hive, carrying it through until the spring cycle freshens the land, providing them with more food and the opportunity to grow the hive again.

It may sound rather random for the small workers to dart from flower to flower, pulling in whatever nectar is out there, but it isn't, really. Bees have brains about the size of a sesame seed, which is large for their size. Scientists have discovered that bees communicate desirable locations, whether for feeding or a new homeplace, through a code—in dance. Their round dance is performed in a figure-eight pattern. A variation called the "waggle dance" is used to describe resources that are even farther from the hive.

Bees also communicate by scent. New queens are created as needed by the workers, who feed the special royal jelly to the larvae that will mature into hive leaders, continuing to eat the special food. The queen bee will make a procession through the hive, leaving her scent trail, rather like a royal procession from medieval times, her scent an assurance that all is well with her—and the hive. When things go wrong in a hive, different scents will arise. An experienced beekeeper may be able to tell from the scent if a hive is getting too worked up to be handled safely and may decide to try again another day.

Drones do not gather nectar or pollen, work it, store honey, build comb, tend the queen and the larvae or defend the hive. They exist solely to mate with the queen—which is a one-time affair. When a new queen is hatched, she will take her "maiden flight," during which all the drones, who have been waiting, buzz around. The successful ones catch her, mate with her one after another and fall to the ground to die, their just-used organs having been ripped from their bodies during the act. The queen, with eggs now hopefully fertilized for the rest of her life, will go into the hive to begin her duties. As for the drones who failed to catch the queen, they linger in the hive until their sisters deem their presence unsupportable, and they are chucked out to die so they will not waste the precious winter stores.

WESTERN BEEKEEPING TRADITIONS FROM ANCIENT TIMES TO THE MIDDLE AGES

H oneybees were maintained by farmers who lived before writing could chronicle their achievements. According to Professor Alan Outram of the University of Exeter, evidence of the use of bee products can be found in sites related to Europe's earliest farmers.

The beekeepers who brought their stocks to Virginia in the seventeenth century and who made studies of them through later centuries were greatly influenced by both tradition and the observations of classical scientists that were recorded in ancient texts and reprinted in proceeding centuries. Both honey and wax were quite useful.

IN ANCIENT TIMES

First find your bees a settled sure abode,
Where neither winds can enter (winds blow back
The foragers with food returning home)…
—*From* Vergil's Georgics, *Book IV*

Bees' society and the products of their industry fascinated and continue to fascinate people, who find them bread (and honey) for philosophical as well as natural studies. Historians have found evidence of early beekeeping

B. Picart invenit et sculpsit 1733.

Hanc olim veteres vitam coluere Sabini   *Scilicet & rerum facta est pulcherrima* ROMA
Hanc Remus & Frater: Sic fortis Etruria crevit   *Virgil. Georg. l. II.*

A celebration party given in honor of a good harvest. Engraving by B. Picart, 1733, after Virgil. *Wellcome Collection. Attribution 4.0 International (CC BY 4.00).*

in cuneiform tablets of the Sumerians and Babylonians. Going back even further, humans working with bees were depicted on the walls of cave-dwellings in the Caves of the Spider (Cuevas de la Araña) in Valencia, Spain.

Honey and other bee products are a real boon to archaeologists, as they can survive under the right conditions. Honey has a tremendous shelf life—and its desirability made it a choice grave good for many cultures. It was found in the tomb of the boy pharaoh Tutankhamun, and even more ancient stores were discovered in a tomb in Georgia, not far from its capital, Tbilisi. The five-thousand-year-old pots contained honey still as sweet and sound as the day it was hidden away from mortal eyes. Archaeologists have found evidence in tombs that the practical ancients used the bees' wax for myriad purposes, including glass and metal casting, waterproofing, candlemaking and cosmetics.

Delightful yet deadly, bees fascinate and inspire. Bees have been kept throughout much of the world, and their stories intertwine with those of the gods and goddesses, from their origin as the fallen tears of the Egyptian god Ra to playing their part alongside the Hindu goddess Parvati on her demon-killing mission.

Ancient Greek and Roman accounts would have been familiar to literate Virginia settlers who had received the benefit of a classical education. Hippocrates (460–377 BC), considered the father of medicine, prescribed honey as an ingredient for remedies treating muscle aches, ulcers and respiratory problems, as well as bee venom to treat arthritis. Today, honey is recognized for its usefulness for cardiovascular, metabolic, immune and anti-inflammatory issues. It has also shown promise as a prebiotic in treating wounds and is considered a "nutraceutical foodstuff" as mentioned in the article "Honey as a Complementary Medicine."

The orderliness of bees inspired the philosopher-scientist Aristotle in his studies of animal life. He kept bees and set down his observations in his *History of Animals*, written about 350 BC. He noted that some people believed that, while the larvae were cared for by the workers, these nurslings were not believed to be created by the bees themselves but found while out foraging for among special flowers, such as those of the olive tree, to be taken back to the hive and tucked away in the comb to be raised by nurse bees.

So it followed, according to that logic, that bees were more likely to increase and then swarm to form new hives when the olives were fertile. Aristotle did note that others believed that bees mated and reproduced in the hive, but the particulars were a little off. In his mind's eye, there was a king bee, or several, who ruled the hive, although too many kings could cause

Hiving bees—scenes from Virgil, Wenceslaus Hollar (1607–1677). *University of Toronto, Wenceslaus Hollar Digital Collection.*

so much splintering in power that the hive would fail. His observations of the bees' work are fascinating to read, even if some of the conclusions are erroneous. Aristotle's studies were passed down to scholars, who commonly understood Greek, and became the basis of natural sciences/biology, where better observations led to more accurate conclusions.

The Roman poet Vergil (or Virgil), writing in book 4 of his *Georgics* in 29 BC, added literary and mythic flourishes to his observations, setting them down in poetic form. He described the little insects' swarms and warfare, while relating the perfect setting for a commodious hive. Book 4 touches on many mythic elements, including Aristaeus, son of Apollo, named by some legends as the first beekeeper, and the theory that bees generated spontaneously from the carcasses of cattle.

Virgil is usually better known for *The Aeneid*, a kind of Roman sequel to Homer's *Iliad* and *Odyssey*. His bees make appearances there, too, as a simile for the industrious followers of Queen Dido and elsewhere in the text. Besides acknowledging Aristaeus, the Greeks also worshipped the Minoan goddess of the bees, Melissa, while the pre-Christian Romans made offerings to Mellona, or Mellonia, their bee and honey goddess. Many other Greco-Roman deities were associated with bees, including Demeter, Aphrodite and Pan.

The Greek mathematician Pythagoras (he of the theorem) also kept bees. His followers, the Pythagorioi, promoted the benefits of bread and honey. Readers with an interest in Western practices of beekeeping in the Greek and Roman period would do well to consult the collection of papers, "Beekeeping in the Mediterranean From Antiquity to the Present," as referenced in this book's bibliography section.

Lucius Junius Moderatus Columella, born in Cadiz, Spain, in the first century AD, retired from his service in the Roman army to take up farming in Italy. His books on farming (*De re rustica*) and trees (*De Arboribus*) survived through the centuries, eventually translated into English and retitled *Of Husbandry* (1745). Beekeeping was naturally one of his subjects. He dutifully acknowledged (and then dismissed) writers before him who dwelt on poetical myths and speculated on the habits of bees and got down to the business of looking after them. His writing would have been very much of interest to colonial farmers and included an early system of moveable frame hives (cuadros móviles), which would continue to be refined in the new country.

Aesop's fables, attributed to a Thracian (modern-day Bulgaria, Greece and Turkey) slave who was born around 620 BC, remain popular stories,

Swarming of bees—scenes from Virgil, Wenceslaus Hollar (1607–1677). *University of Toronto, Wenceslaus Hollar Digital Collection.*

A bear has overturned a beehive and is attacked by bees. Etching by J. Kirk after F. Barlow for a fable by Aesop. *Wellcome Collection. Attribution 4.0 International (CC BY 4.0).*

particularly with young children, as most feature animal characters and teach simple lessons in wisdom. Of course, bees make appearances, as in "The Bear and the Bees":

> *A Bear roaming the woods in search of berries happened on a fallen tree in which a swarm of Bees had stored their honey. The Bear began to nose around the log very carefully to find out if the Bees were at home. Just then one of the swarm came home from the clover field with a load of sweets. Guessing what the Bear was after, the Bee flew at him, stung him sharply and then disappeared into the hollow log. The Bear lost his temper in an instant, and sprang upon the log tooth and claw, to destroy the nest. But this only brought out the whole swarm. The poor Bear had to take to his heels, and he was able to save himself only by diving into a pool of water.*

Above, a bee presents a honeycomb to the Olympian gods in the clouds; below, bees are flying into and out of two wicker beehives. Fable etching by F. Barlow. *Wellcome Collection. Attribution 4.0 International (CC BY 4.0).*

The moral of the story: It is wiser to bear a single injury in silence than to provoke a thousand by flying into a rage. In "The Bee and Jupiter," a bee asks the king of the gods for a death-dealing stinger that will help them protect their hives from humans trying to steal their honey. The bee gets her wish, but with a twist. A honeybee's sting can't be used without tearing out its insides, so its sting is always lethal to the bee. The useful moral here is that evil wishes, like fowls, come home to roost.

These stories were favorites throughout the colonial period. At Kenmore, the home of George Washington's sister in Fredericksburg, Virginia, visitors can see some of Aesop's fables, including "The Fox and the Crow," depicted above the mantel in the Great Room.

But observations as well as charming stories were carried down through the centuries. The Romans Marcus Terentius Varro (116–27 BC) and Pliny the Elder (d. AD 79) wrote of bees' intolerance to people smelling of perfume. Varro, a scholar as well as a beekeeper, had the dubious distinction of having the parasitic Varroa mite, so destructive to a hive, named for him.

Columella's specifics on proper bee stewardship are very much in line with the Stoic philosophy of self-control:

> *Very great care must be taken by the man in charge…when he must handle the hives, that the day before he has abstained from sexual relations, and does not approach them when drunk, and only after washing himself, and that he abstain from all edibles which have a strong flavour.*

The Medieval West

Between the Fall of Rome in the fifth century and the fifteenth-century Renaissance came the medieval period. There were wars, famines, plagues and political and religious upheavals—but there was also the stability of the Church. Having been established during the Roman Empire's later centuries, it maintained centers of learning and encouraged many of its orders to be self-supporting. This included beekeeping, and St. Ambrose (born Aurelius Ambrosius circa AD 340) is the patron saint of beekeepers. Born into a Roman Christian family, Ambrosius became a scholar and later a governor. He tried to refuse the offer to become bishop of Milan but eventually agreed. So, how is he tied to beekeeping? There is a legend that when he was in his cradle, a swarm of bees settled on his face. They left a

St. Ambrose of Milan, patron saint of bees and beekeepers. Unknown artist, circa 1140. Cappella Palatina, Palazzo dei Normanni a Palermo (Sicily, Italy). *Public domain.*

drop of honey in his mouth but did not harm him. This story was used to explain his wonderful way with words.

In the tenth century, during a period known as the Macedonian Renaissance that saw the rise of Byzantine culture, extant wisdom, both current and ancient, on animal husbandry was collected in a volume titled *Geoponika*. Its fifteenth chapter concerned "natural sympathies and antipathies, and of the management of bees." This time was also called the era of Byzantine encyclopedism, as scholars worked to organize knowledge, following the example of their scholar-emperor Constantine VII, who reigned from AD 913 to 959. It does repeat the myth of bees being brought forth from dead oxen, but its advice for where to place a beehive, as well as how to avoid being stung, is of interest:

> *Having poured the juice of wild mallows with oil on the meal of parched fenugreek, and having made it of the consistence of honey, rub your face and the naked parts of your body strenuously; and having swallowed some of it, breathe into the hive three or four times: and having set fire to some cow-dung in a pot, and having brought that to the entrance of the hive, permit the smoke to break in during half an hour, and take and hold the pot at some distance, that the smoke may abound on the outside; and so take the bees.*

Crane and Walker, in their *History of Beekeeping in English Gardens*, detail many particulars of English beekeeping from the twelfth to the nineteenth centuries, a period during which there was not much change.

In the Western medieval period, hives were mostly skeps, made of woven wicker or coiled straw. This is the archetypical beehive with its domed shape. These days, it is mostly ornamental, but a few beekeepers still use it. The English practiced swarm beekeeping. Bees could be counted on to grow their numbers each spring, and the goal was to gather each new swarm in a skep. According to the authors, a beekeeper who had four hives in spring could expect to expand that to twelve after swarming season in May and June. At the end of the season, the heaviest hives—presumably filled with the most honey—were harvested, which necessitated killing the bees. The lightest hives, not expected to be able to survive the winter with their low supplies, were also culled. Hives of medium weight were allowed to continue through another winter.

There are few modern and practical books to be found on skep beekeeping, but Frank Alston's *Skeps: Their History, Making, and Use* is the exception. Alston's interest in skeps grew from his interest in bee boles, the recessed structures, sometimes found built into walls, that housed skeps, protecting them from unfavorable winds and weather. For the early wicker hives themselves (called alvearies), hazel or willow might be woven around stakes to form a dome, then covered over with cloam (or cloom) to keep out the weather—and vermin. Cloom might consist of dung, mixed with lime or ashes to harden it and sand and gravel, which is good against the gnawing of mice. These were in use up until the nineteenth century.

Skeps, crafted from coiled straw or some other reed, were the popular choice before the general use of standardized wooden box hives, dating from roughly the mid-nineteenth century. They were still used by a significant number of traditionalists through the early twentieth century. These days, they may be used for gathering swarms before transfer to a modern hive. The word *skep* seems to derive from the Norse word for a "container" and "basket for grain." The craft of making skeps is called lip work, derived from the Anglo-Saxon word *leáp*, meaning "basket." Alton's book gives specific directions for creating them.

When skeps were still in wide use, skep-making was an extremely useful trade. Skeps did require some additional weatherproofing. A hackle, or coppet, was crafted from long straw, to make a sort of long tent over the skep, providing shelter and insulation. Another kind of cover, the pancheon or creamer, was simply an earthenware vessel used for letting cream settle out from milk at the farm's dairy. Once it was chipped or cracked, it was past its service for the dairy but made a fine protective topper for a beehive. Skep makers also crafted covers that looked rather like simple broad hats.

Making traditional beehives called skeps. *Photo by Michael Reeve, June 27, 2004. CC By SA 3.0.*

Finding very old skeps, due to their construction and use, is a rarity, but free-standing bee shelters and bee boles (shelters recessed within walls) from antiquity can still be found in Britain, as stone is such a lasting substance.

Feudal English estates (post Saxon) consisted of eorls (earls, lords), ceorls (churls, freemen) and serfs, who were not free and usually worked at less skilled tasks on the farm. The eorls held vast properties and important positions. The ceorls might have their own small farms and be craftsmen or have other skills. They served the eorls, and the eorls were expected to protect them and the serfs. According to Alton, the lowest ranking of the ceorls were the beo-ceorl, or beekeeper, and the swineherd. It was usual, upon the beekeeper's death, to pass the position to his son, who would be granted his father's bees. After the Norman succession, the beo-ceorl became known as the custos apium, from the Latin.

Tanging (beating one metal object on another when a swarm emerged) is a custom that dated at least to medieval times. The Anglo-Saxon king Alfred decreed that "every beekeeper must announce the issue of a swarm by ringing bells or clashing metals so it might be followed or captured." According to Alton, a key might be used on a pan or a ploughshare.

Wax was very much valued and had a wide variety of uses, from candles to burial cloths, called cere cloth. Beeswax candles were greatly valued by the Church, and candles play a significant role on Candlemas, also known as the Feast of the Presentation of Jesus Christ. Parishioners bring their next year's supply of candles to be blessed, as Jesus became known as the "Light of the World."

When the English monasteries were dissolved and, in some cases, physically destroyed under Henry VIII's rule, the Church traditions were upended, at least for a time. But before Henry

"Charm wiþ ymbe," Old English charm, from the marginalia of Manuscript 41 at Corpus Christi College (University of Cambridge). *MS 41: Old English Bede (Bedae Historia Saxonice), p. 182. Unknown author. Public domain.*

was even born, the invention of the Gutenberg Press would enable mass printing of books on philosophical subjects as well as the practical, including beekeeping.

The valuable yet unpredictable swarms were the way to multiply a beekeeper's sweet sustenance, but they could escape their domesticity and head to the wild forests and meadows. Beekeepers were not above looking for otherworldly help to keep their workers at home and in the hives.

Two charms or rituals for containing swarming bees have been found in old manuscripts. One seems to be pre-Christian in origin. "For a Swarm of Bees," originally in Anglo-Saxon, was discovered by John Mitchell Kemble in the nineteenth century. In translation, it reads:

> *Against a bee-swarm*
> *Take earth, throw it with your right hand under your right foot and say:*
>
> *I take it under foot; I found it.*
> *Lo! the earth is strong against all kinds of creatures,*
> *and against malice and against forgetfulness*
> *and against the mighty tongue of man.*
>
> *Throw dirt over them when they swarm, and say:*
>
> *Sit, O victory-women, sink to the earth,*
> *never flee, wild to the wood!*
> *Be as mindful of my good*
> *as each man is of food and nation.*

It may be compared with the decidedly plain-spoken Christian prayer to accomplish the same thing by calling on the help of the Holy Ones. Known as the Lorsch Bee Blessing, it is believed to have been written in the ninth century. Here it is translated from High German:

> *Christ, the bee swarm is out here!*
> *Now fly, you my animal, come.*
> *In the Lord's peace, in God's protection,*
> *come home in good health.*
> *Sit, sit bee.*
> *The command to you from the Holy Mary.*
> *You have no vacation;*

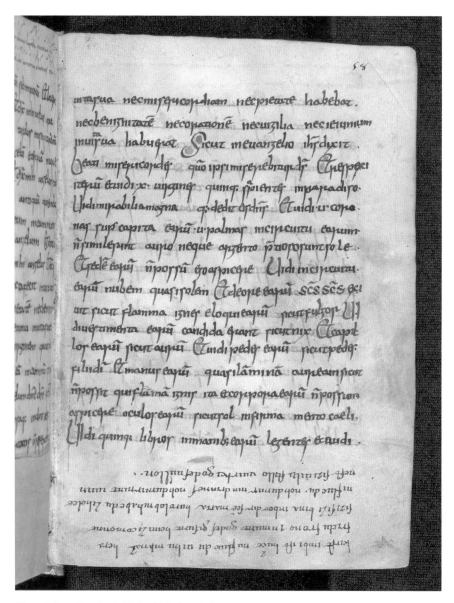

"Lorsch Bee Blessing." Codex Palatinus latinus 220, Fol. 58r, mit dem Lorscher Bienensegen. Biblioteca Apostolica Vaticana, Pal. lat. 220. Unknown author, tenth century. *Public domain.*

Don't fly into the woods;
Neither should you slip away from me.
Nor escape from me.
Sit completely still.
Do God's will.

THE RENAISSANCE AND ENLIGHTENED BEEKEEPERS

Walker and Crane note that early English authors on beekeeping copied from classical writers, adding in their own observations. The first printed English book to mention beekeeping was likely John Fitzherbert's *Book of Husbandry*. He and Thomas Hill, author of *A Profitable Instruction of the Perfect Ordering of Bees*, both mention that gardens were an ideal setting for beehives, as Fitzherbert put it, "kepte from the north wynde, and the mouth of the hyve towarde the sonne."

In addition to bee boles and bee shelters, some beekeepers overwintered their hives in buildings without windows. The buildings' inner walls had spaces for the hives; some were outbuildings, and some stood in gardens.

The gentleman farmer-poet Thomas Tusser gives these instructions (in verse) for setting up a hive in his 1580 book, *Five Hundred Pointes of Good Husbandrie*:

> *Now burne up the bees that ye mind to drive,*
> *at Midsomer drive them and save them alive:*
> *Place hive in good ayer, set southly and warme,*
> *and take in due season wax, honie, and swarme.*
> *Set hive on a plank, (not too low by the ground)*
> *where herbe with flowers may compass it round:*
> *And boards to defend it from north and north east,*
> *from showers and rubbish, from vermin and beast.*

Go look to thy bees, if the hive be too light,
set water and honie, with rosemary dight.
Which set in a dish full of sticks in the hive
from danger of famine yee save them alive.

Take heede to thy bees, that are readie to swarme,
the losse thereof now is a crownes worth of harme:
Let skilfull be readie and diligence seene,
least being too careles, thou losest thy bees.

Saint Mihel byd bees, to be brent out of strife:
Sajnt John bid take honey, with favour of life.
For one sely cottage, set south good and warme:
take body and goodes, and twise yerely a swarme.

Hill makes similar observations on what a hive cannot abide, with a few more particulars for those who love their meat and drink:

The keeper of bees, which mindeth to handle and look into hives, ought the day before to refraine the veneriall Act [sic], *not a person ferefull, nor coming to the hive with unwashed hands and face: and one that ought to refraine in a maner from all smelling meats, poudered meates, fried meates, and all other meates that doe stincke, like as the Leekes, the Onions, the Garlike, and such like, which the Bees greatlie abhorre: besides, to be then sweet of body, cleanlie in apparel, minding to come unto their hives, for in all cleanlinesse and sweetnes the bees are much delighted.*

Bees were respected for their orderliness, so much so that playwright and poet Shakespeare set their hive ways to verse. In his play *Henry V*, the Archbishop of Canterbury uses this speech to convince the king he has the right to France's throne:

The Commonwealth of the Bees

Therefore doth heaven divide
The state of man in divers functions,
Setting endeavor in continual motion;
To which is fixed, as an aim or butt,
Obedience; for so work the honey-bees,

Creatures that, by a rule in nature, teach
The art of order to a peopled kingdom…
The civil citizens kneading up the honey,
The poor mechanic porters crowding in
Their heavy burdens at his narrow gate;
The sad-eyed Justice, with his surly hum,
Delivering o'er to executor pale
The lazy, yawning drone.

The play was written in 1599, just a few years before Elizabeth's relation, the Scots King James, would take the English throne upon her death. Virginia had already been discovered and named for Elizabeth, "the virgin queen," but no permanent English settlements had been established, as the Roanoke Colony was lost in the delays caused by England's war with the Spanish.

Meanwhile, in the German lands, from which many Virginia settlers would come, swarm beekeeping was practiced, as described by Eldingen in his books. He set down much of what he observed and did, including transferring bees to an empty skep by driving them before harvesting their honey, fortifying some hives with honeycombs taken from others and using a cloth to close the mouth of the skep while transporting it. His region, the Lüneburger Heide south of Hamburg, has been famous for its heather honey for centuries. Today, people may visit the German Beekeeping Institute in nearby Celle during their yearly festival to learn more about traditional and modern methods of beekeeping.

With the uptick in printed materials, gentlemen-farmers and literate yeomen could partake of books on farming, distilled from classical authors, with the addition of modern-day observations—and experiments!

Beekeepers were looking for more humane ways to handle their bees, as the standard way of harvesting honey from a traditional skep required killing them with noxious smoke to get at the honey safely.

In 1590, Luigi Alamanni of Florence published *La Coltivazione*, which included Giovanni di Bernardo Rucellai's famous earlier poem, "Le Api" ("The Bees"), describing hives with combs on moveable top bars. Rucellai, a politician as well as a scholar, wrote that piece in the gardens of his family's country estate, considered one of the earliest examples of the Renaissance Italian garden, based on symmetry and imposing order over nature. These gardens would influence those of the French and English and later, the Americans, such as those at the Governor's Palace in Colonial Williamsburg. Interestingly, "Le Api" is a creative reworking of Virgil's *Georgics*.

Melliferis infesti Apibus sunt Papiliones.
Excitat insecti genus hoc Apiarius: & sub

Vase locat noctu flammantia pyramidali
Lumina: eò volitant, flammeaq; ardore necantur.

84.   XXV.

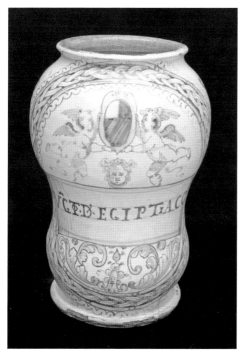

Above: The apiary, circa 1595. The apiary is at right. In the foreground, the bee masters are beating bushes, driving out the moths hidden in them toward flaming lamps set up on the ground. Netherlands. *Cooper Hewitt, Smithsonian Design Museum. Gift of Mrs. A.W. Erickson.*

Left: Drug jar for Egyptian ointment consisting of honey, vinegar and verdigris. Italy, 1585. *Science Museum, London. Attribution 4.0 International (CC BY 4.0).*

In 1609, just two years after Jamestown's initial settlement, Charles Butler, sometimes called "The Father of English Beekeeping," published *The Feminine Monarchie*, the first full-length beekeeping book written in English. Butler's book notes that the bees' leaders and workers were female, while the drones were male—something that had been written of earlier, but Butler's book popularized it. He also observed that wax was produced by workers from within their bodies, rather than being collected from plant materials, as was the usual belief. He shared advice on the safest time to work with hives:

> *If you have anything to doe about your hives, the fittest time is in the morning, when the Bees are new gone abroad; and in the evening before they be come in: for then the weather being coole, and the company few at home, they are not so apt to be quarrelling, unless they be much provoked.*

Charles Butler was born in poverty in Buckinghamshire, but he became a boy chorister at Magdalene College at age eight and eventually completed his studies there. He rose to the position of master of a school but left to accept an incumbency at a rural church in 1600, where he practiced beekeeping, remaining until his passing in 1647.

Sixteenth- and seventeenth-century farming books commonly included sections on beekeeping. *Holinshed's Chronicles* (1586) referred to skeps and why they were made as they were. Spelling in Shakespearean times (and Shakespeare did use Holinshed as a resource for his historical works, according to the British Library) was not so standardized as in modern times:

> *Our hives are made commonlie of rie straw, and wadled about with bramble quarters but some make the same of wicker, and cast them over with claie. Wee…set our hives somewhere on the warmest side of the house, providing that they may stand drie and without danger both of the mouse and moth vicinity of their domicile.*

Also popular were *A Treatise in the Right Use and Ordering of Bees*, by Edmund Southerne (1593), and John Levett's groundbreaking behavioral study, *The Ordering of Bees: Or, The True History of Managing Them* (1634). Historians are still a bit unclear about which John Levett was the author. His sometimes tongue-in-cheek comparisons, such as drones to lawyers, were well received. Mr. Levett, Gentleman, as he signed himself, was one of many, both past and present, to parallel bee society to his own.

Left: Title page for *The Feminine Monarchie, or the Historie of Bees*, by Charles Butler, 1623. *Public domain.*

Right: "The Ordering of Bees, or the True History of Managing Them." Written by John Levett, Gent., published by Thomas Harpur, London, 1634. *Public domain.*

Interestingly, William Lawson's well-known (at the time) *The Country House-Wife's Garden for Herbs of Common Use* includes a section on "the husbandry of bees, with their several uses and annoyances." Women, often caretakers of the kitchen garden, were also frequently the family beekeepers, a tradition that continued in the colonies.

A most remarkable man of the period was Samuel Hartlib (sometimes spelled Hartlieb). His *Reformed Common-wealth of Bees*, bound with *The Reformed Virginian Silk-Worm*, contains "many excellent and choice secrets, experiments, and discoveries for attaining of national and private profits and riches."

Born in Poland and of German extraction, he studied and wrote about numerous fields, including medicine, agriculture, politics and education. He was what is sometimes known as a polymath, with a deep interest and knowledge of numerous fields. He was nicknamed the "Great Intelligencer" for gathering diverse information from scholars of the day through his correspondence. In 1628, he came to England, where he married and eventually came to the attention of Oliver Cromwell, the country's Lord Protector after King Charles's deposition and execution during the English Civil War.

Cromwell and Hartlib saw eye-to-eye in promoting universal education, and the Intelligencer received a yearly stipend for his work. This did not

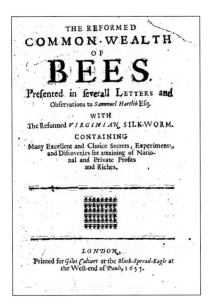

THE REFORMED
COMMON·WEALTH
OF
BEES.
Prefented in feverall LETTERS and
Obfervations to *Samuel Hartlib Efq*.
WITH
The Reformed *VIRGINIAN* SILK-WORM.
CONTAINING
Many Excellent and Choice Secrets, Experiments,
and Difcoveries for attaining of Natio-
nal and Private Profits
and Riches.

LONDON,
Printed for *Giles Calvert* at the *Black-Spread-Eagle* at
the Weft-end of *Pauls,* 1 6 5 5.

The Reformed Commonwealth of Bees, by Samuel Hartlib, 1655. *Public domain.*

make him rich, however, as he spent his money to fund his experiments. He died in poverty, but the majority of his vast correspondence with merchants, refugees, scholars, philosophers and many others, from Transylvania to the English colonies, has been put online by the University of Sheffield, where it may be freely searched and read (https://www.dhi.ac.uk/hartlib/). The letters are considered a treasure-trove of sixteenth- and seventeenth-century literature, and there are numerous references to bees. According to Leigh Penman's 2016 article, "Omnium Exposita Rapinæ: The Afterlives of the Papers of Samuel Hartlib," Hartlib strove to align "all knowledge, physical and metaphysical" and bring about a "reformation, both of Religion, Learning and propagation of the Gospel."

Interest in beekeeping did not slacken with the restoration of Charles II to the throne in 1660. John Gedde's *A New Discovery of an Excellent Method of Bee-houses and Colonies* was "approved by the Royal Society" in London in 1675 and promoted his "new discovery" in keeping beehives. Differently shaped beehives were tried by experimenters and continued to be tried until they became rather standardized in the mid-nineteenth century. Transparent hives were also in vogue among gentlemen-scientists, the better to observe honeybees' interactions. Samuel Pepys noted in his diary on May 5, 1665,

> *After dinner to Mr. Evelings: he being abroad we walked in his garden, and a lovely noble ground he hath endeed. [sic] And among other rarities, a hive of Bees; so, as being hived in glass, you may see the Bees making their honey and combs mighty pleasantly.*

But back to traditional methods, John Reid's practical book *The Scot's… Gard'ner* (1683) gives beekeeping instructions for each month, presumably for skeps, keeping the hive-dwellers snug and fed if necessary as cold weather set its teeth, opening additional passages as spring unfurled, tending to swarms but also to pests and unwanted drones, and finally "taking the bees" (killing

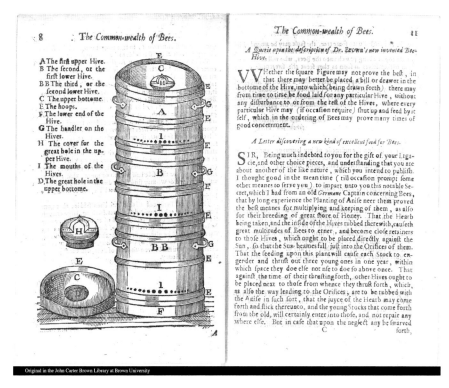

"Bee hive, showing a diagram of its structure and identified as Dr. Thomas Brown's new invented beehive." *The Reformed Commonwealth of Bees*, by Samuel Hartlib, 1655. *JCB Archive of Early American Images.*

them) at the end of the season. In his thoroughness, he also included recipes on how to best use the produce of the garden, and so it is considered the first Scottish cookbook. The online edition referenced in the bibliography has a recipe for metheglin, a kind of honey wine, on pages 176–77.

Reid's book also contains instructions for raising Virginia tobacco, which was a tricky proposition due to the differences in climate. However, tobacco was readily available in Virginia itself, and many beekeepers smoked tobacco. By puffing mouthfuls of smoke onto the bees, they dulled the insects' senses with its narcotic effect, making them easier to handle. By the early 1700s, separate smokers were invented, allowing beekeepers to achieve the same effect without the health risk—although, according to Crane's *World History of Beekeeping and Honey Hunting*, they were used mostly where beekeeping operations were done in a bee house, such as Germany, Austria, German-speaking Switzerland, parts of Czechoslovakia and Poland, Alsace (now in France) and the Netherlands.

Women were regarded as natural beekeepers, as they kept the home and its garden, as well as its stillroom, source of many a remedy. In the article "The History of Beekeeping in English Gardens," in the journal *Garden History*, the authors remark that from the late sixteenth century, some English authors assumed that country women cared for both garden and bees. One author addressed his instructions to "good conie"—*conie* being a term of endearment for a woman. William Lawson's *The Country Housewife's Garden*, written in 1621, includes a chapter on "The Husbandry of Bees":

> *I will not account her any of my good Housewives, that wanteth either Bees or skilfulnesse about them....You must have an house made along, a sure dry wall in your Garden, neere, or in your Orchard: for Bees love Flowers and wood with their hearts.*

IMMIGRANT BEES

Bees existed in North America before the European colonists brought them over the ocean. But they weren't honeybees. The native bees did their pollination job perfectly well—mason bees in particular are considered important pollinators that should be encouraged. Among the many other species are mining bees, sweat bees, plasterer or masked bees— and, of course, the bumblebee. But *Apis mellifera*, the European honeybee, has been semi-domesticated for so long and provides useful stuff in the way of honey and wax, that naturally settlers would want them—and so did the powers providing the funding for the Virginia colony.

Several historical writers, including John Eliot, writing in 1661, and later president Thomas Jefferson, noted that the native people had no word for honeybees, or honey or beeswax for that matter. They called the escaped swarms, of which there were many, "white men's flies" and knew that if they saw them, settlements could not be far behind.

As an aside, there is a kind of stingless honeybee (the Melipona) in the Western Hemisphere—but not outside the warmer regions. The *Melipona beecheii* are native to the Yucatán Peninsula in Mexico and were cultivated by the Mayans thousands of years ago. There are some distinct differences between the Melipona and the European honeybee. The stingless (although they will bite to protect their colony) cousin does not produce honeycomb— and therefore no wax. It also makes far less honey, although the taste is quite pleasant. But with its preference for a tropical climate—some colonies have been successfully started in Cuba—this species would be a nonstarter in colonial Virginia, even if it had been generally known. According to Pryor's *Honey, Maple Sugar and Other Farm Produced Sweeteners in the Colonial Chesapeake*, the stingless varietal had managed to establish itself as far as Florida and Georgia by the sixteenth century.

ACROSS THE ATLANTIC

The Virginia Company was responsible for financing the colony's progress. Not surprisingly, it wished to reap a profit after paying for expenses. Growing the colony required innovative supplies. On December 5, 1621, the Council of the Virginia Company, based in London, sent a letter to the governor and council in Virginia:

> We have by this ship *The Discovery* sent you divers sorts of seeds, and fruit trees, as also pidgeons, connies [rabbits], peacocks, mastiffs, and beehives, as you shall by the invoice perceive; the preservation & increase whereof we respond unto you.

Luke Dixon, in his *Keeping Bees in Towns and Cities*, notes that bees were considered wild creatures in England and were simply in the custody of keepers, as opposed to the way beekeeping has come to be seen in the United States, where they are considered chattel, or moveable possessions, much the same as cattle, sheep and horses.

The Discovery and its sister ships, the *Bona Nova* and the *Hopewell*, arrived in Virginia in March 1622 with their useful cargo—the mastiffs to provide protection, the coneys to be a quick source of meat and fur and the beehives to house the industrious providers of honey and wax.

It seems most likely the bees were shipped in skeps, and as the passage took place in the winter, they were likely dormant. With a moving vessel constantly changing the bees' position relative to the sun, their own navigation would likely be confused. For later crossings made in warmer months, the hives could be kept near ice, to achieve an artificial dormancy, making them easier to handle.

In 1985, John Adams and D.A. Smith "visited the place where the ships unloaded their cargoes: a wharf (no longer existing) under a bluff where the Appomattox River flows into the James. The town is now called Hopewell, and a nearby farm had previously been named Hopewell after the ship," as noted in Eva Crane's *The World History of Beekeeping and Honey Hunting*.

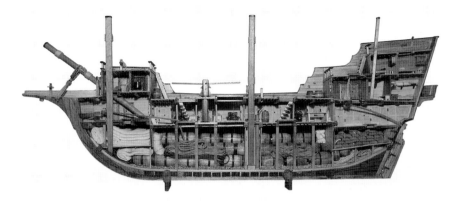

Model of a seventeenth-century English merchantman ship of about four hundred tons. Dorset County Museum. *Image by user Musphot on Wikimedia Commons.*

Why such a late start for bees, since they were known to be so useful? The story behind that is tied together with a shipwreck and the genesis of one of Shakespeare's most enjoyed plays. In June 1609, England's first purpose-built emigrant ship, the *Sea Venture*, began its voyage to Jamestown. It was the flagship of the "Third Supply Relief Fleet," whose vessels carried approximately five hundred colonists, including John Rolfe and his first wife—Rolfe was later to marry the Native princess known to history as Pocahontas.

At the end of July, with the voyage not over, a hurricane sank one ship and threw the *Sea Venture* onto a reef near Bermuda. All 150 of the ship's passengers were saved, at least initially, from the wreck, but the *Sea Venture* was carrying most of the food supplies needed for the starving colony at Jamestown, as well as hives of bees. The seven smaller ships did arrive at Jamestown, but without the bulk of needed provisions and even more mouths to feed in the way of new colonists. Jamestown's Starving Time began in November of that same year.

By February 1610, the castaways had used wood from the *Sea Venture* coupled with wood they found at Bermuda to build two ships, the *Deliverance* and the *Patience*. When they eventually arrived at Jamestown, again short on supplies from having to consume them, they were met by 60 survivors from the Starving Time of the 240 original colonists. Loaded aboard the *Deliverance* and the *Patience*, the survivors of both the shipwreck and Jamestown Colony were prepared to retreat to England. However, before they were well underway, they met ships bearing a new governor and a year's worth of supplies. They returned to James Fort. The Jamestown Colony would continue. The bees, however, having escaped their hives on sunny Bermuda, started their new colonies elsewhere.

One of the survivors of the wreck, William Strachey, penned a well-written account of the wreck and its aftermath in the form of a letter. It bears striking similarities in its descriptions to Shakespeare's *The Tempest*, written in 1611, and another passenger's account, *A Discovery of the Barmudas, Otherwise Called the Ile of Divels*, could have provided additional inspiration.

A Valuable Addition

Even if a lot of bees were lost in transit, once they were established in the colony, they multiplied by swarming very readily.

According to Cotter and Hudson in "New Discoveries at Jamestown," candles were the most common lighting device in early Jamestown, usually made from either tallow, a shelf-stable animal fat, or bayberry wax, the latter being wonderfully sweet-smelling but time-consuming to devise, as bayberries provide only a small amount of wax. Pine torches might be used outdoors, while rushlights (the dried pith of the rush plant dipped in tallow) and candlewood (pine knots taken from fat pitch pine) were used in humble dwellings.

Richard Bradley (1688–1732), an English botanist, urged colonists to raise bees as "they cost nothing to maintain, and prosper exceedingly where they have such Benefits (as flowers); therefore in such places they should not be wanting, for their Wax and Honey amount to a good Value."

Beeswax, readily available from the hive, was tremendously helpful for people living with few affordable stores near them. It was also quite a profitable export. Bill Krebs, who served as a volunteer beekeeper when Colonial Williamsburg maintained that program, discovered in his research that between 1740 and 1744, Yorktown, Virginia—not a large town—exported eight thousand pounds of beeswax.

There were some other sweeteners available to early colonists, but none was as familiar to them as honey. Maples are traditionally tapped from mid-February to mid-March as the sap begins to flow. Any type of maple may be used, but sugar maples will yield the most syrup from the same amount of sap. Today, the producers in Virginia's mountain regions have devised a Maple Syrup Trail to help visitors find their way to the sugar camps and festivals.

The thorny honey locust tree, not to be confused with the black locust, has pods that produce a substance that could be used as a sweetener. Cornstalks could be crushed to yield a sweet syrup, and, by the end of the colonial period, some farmers had begun to experiment with this early corn syrup. In time, cane sugar from West Indian plantations became popular toward the end of the seventeenth century, and molasses, its byproduct, began to take the place of honey in a significant way. But the molasses trade had issues, including its reliance on enslaved labor. The Molasses Act of 1733 sought to protect the profits of British-run sugar plantations in the West Indies by taxing molasses imports from non-British colonies, such as the French West Indies. The American colonists objected to this act, as the British West Indies could not provide enough molasses to keep up with the demand for New England's rum production. Smuggling was the usual workaround, and American colonists' pique at the Sugar Act of 1764 would inspire revolutionary thoughts.

As noted in *Planters of Colonial Virginia*, honey was abundant for personal use, and there were few householders who did not have hives under the eaves of their outbuildings. One planter, George Pelton, also known as George Strayton, is said to have made a profit of thirty pounds from his bees. Writing in the early eighteenth century, Robert Beverley noted that "bees thrive there abundantly, and will very easily yield to the careful Huswife, two Crops of Honey in a Year, and besides lay up a Winterstore sufficient to preserve their Stocks." There was more difficulty in harvesting from wild bees, however they might exist in a kind of Eden:

> *Of spontaneous Flowers they have an unknown Variety: The finest Crown Imperial in the World; the Cardinal-Flower, so much extoll'd for its Scarlet Colour, is almost in every Branch; the Moccasin Flower, and a Thousand others, not yet known, to English Herbalists. Almost all the Year round, the Levels and Vales are beautified with Flowers of one Kind or other, which make their Woods as fragrant as a Garden. From these Materials their wild Bees make vast Quantities of Honey, but their Magazines are very often rifled, by Bears, Raccoons, and such like liquorish Vermine.*

AT THE APOTHECARY AND IN THE HOME

From ancient times until the present day, honey has been a key component of many medicines, and it was certainly in use during Virginia's early history. Whether to make a sometimes-noxious preparation more palatable or serving to soothe throats, as it still does, honey would be the physician's and the patient's friend. Sometimes, as in the case of Dr. Hugh Mercer of Fredericksburg, a physician might keep his own apothecary, where medicines could be mixed to the doctor's prescription. Costumed guides in a re-creation of Dr. Mercer's shop welcome visitors while good-humoredly divulging what sort of unique remedies might be required for ailments of the day. These range from reusable pills (!) to bloodletting leeches and opium tinctures. Two out of three of these are still in use. In a town of some size, an educated doctor in a town, such as Scotsman Hugh Mercer, was often a well-regarded member of colonial society. Having some wealth, an apothecary would usually have servants, including enslaved persons, who could help prepare his medicines and treat the ill.

Dr. John De Sequeyra, a Jewish physician, practiced medicine in Williamsburg beginning about 1745. He was born in London in 1712 and studied at Leiden University in Holland, graduating in 1739. He was friends with other local physicians and treated Lord Botetourt in his last illness and was appointed visiting physician to Williamsburg's hospital for the insane. When De Sequeyra died in 1795, Richmond newspapers described him as "an eminent famous physician."

Dr. De Sequeyra left behind a fascinating essay on ailments suffered during the latter half of the eighteenth century. He mentioned one of several remedies to try for a high fever accompanying something frequently fatal to children called the Rotten-Quinsey: "Gargles of Tinctures of Roses & Myrrh with honey of Roses sufficiently acidulated with sweet spirit of nitre." According to historian Harold B. Gill, Rotten-Quinsey may have been diptheria, a standard object for modern childhood vaccination.

Sir John Hill, an eighteenth-century London apothecary (as well as playwright, actor, novelist and journalist) wrote *The Family Herbal*, in which he included a recipe for Honey of Roses:

> *Cut the white heels from some red rose buds, and lay them to dry in a place where there is a draught of air; when they are dried, put half a pound of them into a stone jar, and pour on them three pints of boiling water; stir them well, and let them stand twelve hours; then press off the liquor (liquid) and when it has settled, add to it five pounds of honey; boil it well, and when it is of the consistence of thick syrup, put it by for use. It is good against mouth sores, and on many other occasions.*

Narbonne Honey.

THE Late Dr. FOTHERGILL, having conſtantly recommended NARBONNE HONEY to be Eat
on Toaſted Bread, during the Winter Months for Break-
faſt, as being particularly Wholeſome, preventing Coughs,
Colds, Fevers, Conſumptions, &c.

Mr. THORLEY,

HONEY MERCHANT

To HER MAJESTY, and the ROYAL FAMILY,

At the KING's ARMS, No. 40, *New-Bond-Street*,
And at No. 29, *Lombard-Street*;

BEGS Leave to inform the PUBLIC, that he has juſt
Landed out of the *Hector*, from *France*, a Quantity of
Genuine NARBONNE HONEY, which is now
put into ſmall Jars, and ſold at both of his Shops.

The peculiar Virtues of this fragrant Honey, in relieving
all Complaints of the Breath and Lungs, make it of ſuch
Value, that many Perſons ſell it adulterated.

☞ A Bill of our Shop will be delivered with each Jar.

N. B: Our GRAND APIARY for BEES, at *Walthamſtow*, may
be ſeen by our Cuſtomers (Gratis) in the Summer Months.

*** *Engliſh and Foreign Honey of all Sorts.*

Left: Narbonne honey...: as being particularly wholesome, preventing coughs, colds, fevers, consumptions, &c. Early 18th century. *Public domain.*

Below: Colonial Williamsburg Virginia Apothecary Medicine Shop. *watts_photos (CC BY 2.0).*

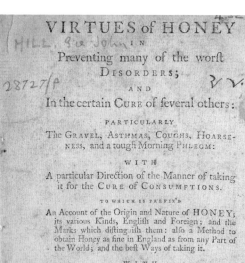

Above: Colonial Williamsburg Virginia Apothecary Medicine Shop. *watts_photos (CC BY 2.0)*.

Left: *The Virtues of Honey in Preventing Many of the Worst Disorders; and in the Certain Cure of Several Others: Particularly the Gravel, Asthmas, Coughs, Hoarseness, and a Tough Morning Phlegm: With a Particular Direction...for the Cure of Consumptions, etc.* by John Hill, 1760. *Wellcome Collection.* *Public domain.*

[50]

IF there be any perfon whom the fineft Honey difagrees with, as I have feen one or two, whofe conftitution feemed to have a natural antipathy to it, I have always found that the mixing with the Honey, a very fmall quantity of powder of cinnamon prevented this entirely.

CHAP. XIII.

Of Syrup of Capillaire.

THE Capillaire fo celebrated for coughs and diforders of the breaft, derives its virtue, in a manner entirely, from the Honey. Many idle receipts have been publifhed for the making it, but the Italian kind which is fineft of all, is no more than this. Pick from the ftalks four ounces of frefh leaves of the true maidenhair, while they are young, and without feeds. Pour u₁on thefe a quart of boiling water. Let it ftand eighteen hours; then filter it through paper, add to this four pounds of pure Honey. Boil this a few minutes and then

Honey recipe. Syrup of Capillaire. For coughs. From *The Virtues of Honey* by John Hill, 1760. *Wellcome Collection. Attribution 4.0 International (CC BY 4.0).*

Sir John was also renowned for his Pectoral Balsam of Honey. It was composed of balsam of tolu (a plant resin), opium, honey and spirit of wine. He began producing such patent remedies around the 1760s, which greatly enriched his purse, which had been depleted by his other publishing efforts. The Pectoral Balsam of Honey was widely advertised as "the unequalled efficacy and safety of this elegant Medicine in the immediate relief, and gradual cure, of Coughs, Colds, Sore Throats, Hoarseness, Difficulty of Breathing, Catarrhs, Asthma, and Consumptions."

Unlike most patent remedies, Balsam of Honey had staying power. In March 1845, an advertisement appeared in the *Alexandria Gazette* for Hance's Compound Medicated Horehound Candy—"For Coughs, Colds, Spitting of Blood, Asthma, Sore Throat, Clearing the Voice, Consumption, Bronchitis, Croup, &c."

This celebrated CANDY is a scientific and medical compound; therefore to avoid all appearance of quackery, and at the same time remove an objection that some persons have to take a medicine of which the ingredients are held a secret from them, it has been thought proper to mention the principle medicines which enter into its composition.

THIS VEGETABLE CANDY IS COMPOSED OF THE FOLLOWING INGREDIENTS:

Horehound, Wild Cherry, Senagal Root, Boneset, Irish Moss, Comfrey Root, Gum Arabic, Balsam Tolu, Gum Benzoni, Liverwort, Iceland Moss, Elecampaine, Squills, Coltsfoot, Flaxseed, Slippery Elm, Faragorie, Balsam of Honey, AND OTHER INGREDIENTS, AMOUNTING TO TWENTY-SEVEN. Price 25 cents per package, or five for $1.

Patent medicines, drawn from folk remedies, continued to be widely advertised through the 1800s and into the 1900s:

Dr. Von Senden's
Fennel Honey Extract
POSITIVELY CURES ALL AFFECTIONS OF THE LUNGS,
THROAT AND CHEST,
SUCH AS COUGHS, COLDS, &C.
FOR SALE BY ALL DRUGGISTS. Try it. It never fails.
25 and 50 cents per bottle.
THEO. HINRICHS, Apothecary, Washington.
W. FRANKLIN CREIGHTON.
Wholesale Agt. Alexandria, Va.
—printed in the Alexandria Gazette, *November 30, 1882*

Often far from town and frequently short on funds, farmers' wives and farmers themselves relied on home remedies for many illnesses. An herb garden not only supplied savory flavors for the table but also proved to be a real help in creating comforts for the sick. Recipes for home concoctions sometimes appeared in newspapers:

A receipt to clean the teeth and gums, and make flesh grow close to the root of the enamel.
TAKE an ounce of myrrh in fine powder, two spoonfuls of the best white honey, and a little green sage in fine powder; mix them well together, and rub the teeth and gums with a little of this balsam every night and morning.
—Virginia Gazette, *January 28, 1773*

SORE TONGUE IN HORSES
As there is a fatal disease among the horses in this neighborhood, at this time, called sore tongue, and as I have obtained the following recipe for curing it, I deem it right to send it to you, in order that you may make it public to benefit those who may have horses so diseased. —Centreville, Va., August 17, 1846. ——Alexandria Gazette, *August 22, 1846*

Honey was a part of that equine remedy, likely to make the medicine more tolerable, as some of the other components were alum, red oak bark, "and a small quantity of red pepper."

Almanacs, with their advice on planting by the signs of the zodiac, were popular with farmers and planters—and another place to find medical advice. The *Virginia Almanack* for 1768 included treatments for coughs and consumption and claimed that honey was crucial in a cure for the ill effects of drinking cold water when overheated.

Beekeeping at Chelsea Physic Garden, London. *Sue Snell. Attribution 4.0 International (CC BY 4.0).*

One ethnic group that settled throughout the Shenandoah Valley in the 1700s, the Germans, came mostly by way of Pennsylvania. They brought their folk healing traditions, which naturally included herbs and honey, with them. In his article "The Folk Medicine of the Pennsylvania Dutch," David Cohen lists remedies, including this "cure" for tuberculosis:

> *The householder could take two handfuls of fennel seed, two of anise seed, and one handful each of liquorice, angelica, senna leaves, lungwort, white sage, hyssop, crowfoot, and two other herbs, put them together in an earthen pot, pour four quarts of water on them, cook a third of it, then strain and add two tablespoons of honey.*

In another publication, *Folk Medicine of the Pennsylvania Germans*, a hot poultice consisting of breadcrumbs and honey is mentioned as a way to bring out the poison (pus) from boils or carbuncles. An inflamed mouth might be treated with products of the hive: "Take a chicken egg, honey, and alum, of each the size of a walnut; heat, stir, and then use to smear." Honey was also part of treatments for scurvy; clearing the throat for public speaking, either on its own or made into mustard and honey cakes; and

The Bee Friend (German, *Der Bienenfreund*), Hans Thoma (1839–1924). Staatliche Kunsthalle Karlsruhe. *Public domain.*

"Bee-keeper," copy from a German stained-glass picture of 1753. *Ingeborg Bernhard. (Schnorch). Attribution 4.0 International (CC BY 4.0).*

used directly on children's backs overnight to draw out the "spine worm." To avoid gangrene or infection ("poison in the blood"), an injury might be dressed with honey mixed with sharp soap, after which, "one can wait with security the coming of the surgeon."

Modern folk medicine embraces local honey for taming seasonal allergies, among other possible uses. However, the National Center for Complementary and Integrative Health, part of the U.S. Government's National Institutes of Health, looked at the few studies done on honey's connection to seasonal allergies, and as of this writing, their findings were inconclusive. The center also stresses that honey should never be given to children under the age of one because of risks associated with botulism.

THE LURE OF WILD HONEY

Honey has been hunted for millennia, according to evidence found on the walls of caves in Valencia, Spain. The Cuevas de la Araña, or the Spider Caves, has an image of a person apparently pulling honey from a treetop hive while bees hover nearby; the figure has a bucket in hand to collect it.

According to Pryor, colonists might take wild bees for their own by capturing a swarm in a new hive with a lure of sweet-smelling herbs or sugar water. But many a colonist took the hollowed-out tree with the bees in it during autumn, thus keeping the honey and comb already made along with the bees.

St. John (or Jean) de Crèvecœur (1735–1813), whose full name was Michel Guillaume Jean de Crèvecœur, was a minor French nobleman who later became a naturalized American citizen, after having served on the opposing side in the French and Indian War. He was an avid farmer and beekeeper who also enjoyed hunting bees. His method was to attract them to a pool of honey, dyed a bright red, by lighting a beeswax candle. Once the bees marked themselves in the honey pool, he was able to follow them more easily back to their hives. He used a compass and a watch to better chart them as they returned to their hives. This charting came naturally to him, as he had served as a military cartographer. Watching the path the bees took was called "bee lining," and it was used by many country dwellers to find a hive. Bee hunting was a profitable venture, whether taking the part of their hollowed-out tree home with bees and honey intact or just smoking out the bees and taking honey on its own.

"Robbing a Wild Bee Hive," *Harpers Weekly*, November 3, 1883. *Public domain.*

If the haul from a bee tree was particularly large, Crèvecœur (or, rather his wife, Mehitable Tippet, the daughter of a New York merchant) made mead from the takings. He believed their mead was particularly delicious because Mehitable included "two gallons of brandy in each barrel, which ripens it, and takes off that sweet, luscious taste, which is apt to retain a long time." Such a brew is called fortified mead.

Those wishing to look more into early American honey hunting may want to read one of James Fenimore Cooper's lesser-known works, *Oak Openings, or The Bee Hunter* (see the bibliography for an online copy). Published in 1848, the novel gives a detailed account of honey hunting as it was done in 1812 by Cooper's main character, Benjamin Boden, nicknamed Ben Buzz.

Honey hunting was very much enjoyed throughout the nineteenth century. *Harper's Weekly*, a wildly popular magazine of the period, ran a cheery feature on "Robbing a Wild-Bee Hive," which follows the much the same method:

"Bee-hunting," writes an enthusiast, "is the poetry of sport." The rich, warm days of September afford the best season for the sport, as then the bees are compelled to roam far and wide in search of food, as the honey-bearing flowers are nearly gone. The first thing in bee-hunting is to catch your bee. Practiced hunters capture a little forager in a box with a glass lid, in which a little bit of honey-comb is inclosed [sic]. After Mr. Bee has taken his fill, he is allowed to escape. He rises a few feet in the air, circles round two or three times, and then makes a bee-line home. If the tree in which the hive has taken up its abode is within half a mile, the bee usually returns in a short time, and brings with him two or three friends, to whom he has communicated the interesting fact that he has found a box of honey. In a short time a line of bees may be established. But in many instances a second line has to be established. A second base of operations is selected some distance from the first, another bee caught, dismissed, and traced.

Then, where the two lines meet, the hunter may be sure the prize is not far distant. The inexperienced sportsman is troubled at first with the difficulty of tracing the little wanderer. In some countries the hunter attaches some white cottony substance to the bee, which makes it more conspicuous as well as slower in its flight. Some experts sprinkle the captive with flour, others with sulphur, before he is released from the trap to wing his homeward flight, and become an involuntary betrayer of his queen and the body-politic. The sulphur sprinkling is said to set the bees in a perfect uproar, so that they can be followed by ear as well as by eye. The tree in which the nest is located is usually an old one, with the top more or less decayed. To obtain the honey, the tree is in most instances felled, and then, if it is much decayed, the comb is badly broken and much of the honey is wasted. The bees, at the first stroke of the axe, would pour forth, ready to make war on everything, unless due precautions are taken.

The wisest plan, therefore, is to stop up all openings but one, and smoke the insects out; a puff of tobacco soon deadens them and renders them harmless. The honey-bee of the woods is the same as the honey-bee of the farm, and has arisen from swarms that have flown away from civilization. The rapidity with which they increase is almost incredible: one swarm has been known to produce twenty-two during a single season. In Texas, they have been seen pouring out in streams as thick as a man's body. We have said the fall is the best time for hunting bees, as the hive is then full of honey, but bee trees are sometimes discovered in the bright days of early spring, while the ground is still covered with snow. The warmth of the sun attracts the bees out of their hiding-place, but they are blinded by the glare of the snow, and may be found lying on the ground near the entrance to their retreat. In the wooded and mountainous districts the number of wild swarms is very large. In the north they often perish before the spring, but in the more genial regions multiply and flourish.

Wild honey was a very desirable food. Warren White Sulphur Springs advertised the opening of its "pleasant mountain retreat" in a July 1859 issue of the *Alexandria Gazette*. They promised "the best provisions and delicacies of the season from the Washington and Alexandria markets, such as Crabs, Turtles, Fish, etc., besides supplies of Mutton, Wild Honey, etc. from the markets of the valley and mountains adjacent to the Springs."

The *Richmond Planet*, an African American newspaper, frequently ran articles on beekeeping, but in the October 25, 1902 issue, it featured "The Finding of Honey," giving the established protocol for dealing with bee trees, such as marking them for future use.

Sweet Poison

Not all found honey was desirable or even healthy. In 1802, B. Barton gave an account of "the Poisonous and Injurious Honey of North America." Here is an excerpt, with spelling adjusted for more modern eyes:

> *In July of the year 1785, I had an opportunity of observing some of the disagreeable effects of our wild honey upon several persons who had eaten of it, in the western parts of Pennsylvania, near the river Ohio.…The honey which I call deleterious or poisonous honey produces, as far as I have learned, the following symptoms and effects; in the beginning a dimness of sight or vertigo, succeeded by a delirium, which is sometimes mild and pleasant and sometimes ferocious…pain in the stomach and intestines, convulsions, profuse perspiration, foaming at the mouth, vomiting, and purging; and in a few instances, death.…Sometimes the honey has been observed to produce a temporary palsy of the limbs, an effect which I have remarked, in animals that have eaten of one of those very vegetables from whose flowers the bees obtain a pernicious honey.…*

Possible dangers of consumption aside, honey hunting continued to be a fine sport—if only for the onlookers. The following article, which appeared in the September 20, 1910 issue of the *Virginia Gazette* tells a cautionary tale:

> *"Taking a Bee Tree at Roxbury"*
>
> *Roxbury, Va., Aug. 29. This little town was thrown into a state of excitement a few nights ago when about 10 o'clock several shots were heard some distance from this place and cries for help went out on the still midnight air that made those who were awake get busy and those who had retired early wake up badly frightened. It seems several young men had located a bee tree on the land of a farmer who never allows a tree to be cut. At 8 o'clock Messrs. C.D. Binns, the young merchant at this place, and Mr. Williams the new operator who is filling the position for Mr. J.G. McCann, who is off for 30 days, and young Whit Tun-stall and Eddie Adams with bucket, light and ax, started to get the honey. Young Williams was put in a position to watch for the land owner. A certain signal was to let the choppers know so they might escape. All went along nicely.*
>
> *When the tree was about to fall, three shots were fired in quick succession close to Young Williams. "Mur-der, murder!" were the first words spoken*

by Young Williams. "Please do not kill me, for my mother's sake." Young Williams tried to run, but got entangled in a briarpatch, then a barb wire fence, being a stranger in a strange place, followed by an irate farmer. The young man's cries were pitiful in the extreme. He was left by his frightened friends, as he supposed, to die. After the excitement was over, and a three hours search, Young Williams was found lying face down in the briars. His prayers for deliverance would have done credit to any preacher. The sight was a frightful one, as the young man's clothes were torn to shreds, hands and face lacerated and bleeding, all done by the cruel briars and barb wire. Now SAY HONEY or BEE TREE to Young Williams, and it's a foot race or a fight.

BEES ON FARMS–AND PLANTATIONS

On Farms

Researchers rarely find mention of beehives in wills or inventories in the Chesapeake Bay area of the seventeenth century. But, as noted by Pryor, that may be misleading, as many farmers would keep their bees in hollow logs (bee gums) or old boxes that might be lumped under old lumber or not counted at all. Beehives were documented more frequently at wealthier estates, but that might be because their hives were more obviously purpose-built. The ready availability of wild honey to meet immediate needs probably hindered the deliberate growth of apiculture. Wild bees often made their homes in black gum trees, called bee gums for the way they readily hollowed out as they aged, leaving a comfortable home for the bees, as described in Colonial Williamsburg's "Bees in the Colonies" podcast. The bee gums would be cut off to a size of three feet, plugged at one end entirely with a restricted entrance at the other, and that made a rather natural beehive with no special skep-making skill required.

In Robert Beverley's 1722 book, *The History of Virginia, in Four Parts*—granted a kind of advertisement for future colonists—his chapter on natural products and the "Advantages of Husbandry" speaks to the probable beekeepers, the women:

> *Bees thrive there abundantly, and will very easily yield to the careful Huswife a full Hive of Honey, and besides lay up a Winter-store sufficient to preserve their Stocks.*

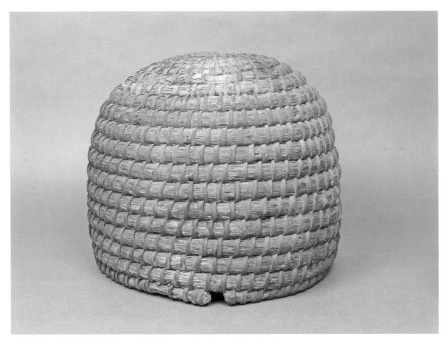

Skep (beehive basket), maker unknown. Probably Shenandoah Valley, late nineteenth or early twentieth centuries, rye grass. *Collection of the Museum of the Shenandoah Valley, 2001.0013.213.*

Homes, or rather homesteads, of early farmers tended to be modest in size and plain in design. The best of them were snug and comfortable in their way. Few survived through the centuries, as they were not showplaces like Stratford Hall or Ash Lawn or Monticello, and fewer still can be found today. Suburban growth in past decades has covered old farmlands with single-family houses, townhouses and shopping areas.

But the curious can still visit a few humbler places, such as the Ball-Sellers House in Arlington County, first built as a log cabin by yeoman farmer John Ball. In England, a yeoman—a term dating back centuries—was a free-born person who likely owned his own land. Socially, he was above a regular husbandman, who might tend flocks and herds, but below the landed gentry. In England, yeomen were expected to fill the ranks of the military services in times of war, and a naval rank was named for them. The English yeomen archers made history at the Battle of Agincourt, among other places, and made legends as part of Robin Hood's merry band of outlaws.

Originally seated on 166 acres granted in 1742 by Lord Fairfax (for whom Fairfax County is named), the cabin was made from logs John Ball felled

Ball-Sellers House, Arlington, Virginia. *Photo by mebrett. CC BY 2.0*

and notched, chinking the cracks with mud daubing. He lived with his wife, Elizabeth, and five daughters. In time, he added a lean-to and covered the structure with clapboard, giving it a less rustic appearance. According to his estate's inventory, he raised wheat and corn and kept sheep, pigs, cows and bees, although there are none on site at present. He also ran a mill to grind his corn and wheat and that of his neighbors.

The Enlightenment of the seventeenth and eighteenth centuries touched the self-sufficient yeomen class, expanding their horizons. John Ball passed in 1766, but his fellow yeomen would fill the ranks of the Continental army, trading bows for muskets.

Yeomen farmers, now American citizens, maintained their taste for self-sufficiency. Newspapers frequently carried suggestions on how to use readily available substances, such as beeswax from the garden hive, to improve daily life. This short post, reprinted from *The American Farmer* in a local Virginia paper, details how to handle a seasonal problem:

The New England fishermen preserve their boots tight against water by the following method, which it is said, has been in use among them one hundred years: A pint of boiled linseed oil, half a pound of mutton suet, six ounces of clean beeswax and four ounces of rosin, are melted and well mixed over a fire. Of this, while warm, not so hot as may burn the leather, with a brush lay plentifully on new boots or shoes, when they are quite dry and clean. The leather is left pliant. Fishermen stand in their boots thus prepared in water, hour after hour without inconvenience. For three years past, all my shoes, even of calf skin, have been so served; and have, in no instance, admitted water to pass through the leather.
—Genius of Liberty, *January 21, 1823*

Farmers might use some of their honey to make the warming (and alcoholic) beverage mead. Occasionally, farmers also used honey to make metheglin, a flavored and perhaps spiced mead. Elizabeth Pryor, in her work on colonial Chesapeake farmers, shared this recipe from the period:

Take eight Gallons of Water, and as much Honey as will make it bear an Egg; add to this the Rind of six Lemmons, and boil it well, scumming it carefully as it rises. When 'tis off the Fire, put to it the juice of the six Lemmons, and pour it into a clean Tub, or open earthen Vessel, if you have one large enough, to work three Days; then scum it well, and pour off the clear into the Cask, and let it stand open till it has done making a hissing Noise; after which, stop it up close, and in three months' time it will be fine, and fit for bottling.

TROUBLE IN THE HIVE

Thriving though they might be, bees were not able to merrily go on their way and make and store honey unhindered. Birds, such as sparrows and swallows, found them delicious game. The Reverend John Thorley advised shooting the winged hunters or setting traps for them. He also recommended crushing spiders and destroying their webs, as they might catch bees in flight. Honey-seeking mice might be kept at bay by making the hive entrance too small for them and setting the hive on an impermeable block.

The ever-observant Crèvecœur stood by as a kingbird ate 171 bees. He struck the bird down, opened its craw and placed the bees on a cloth to be warmed by the sun. This was an effective treatment, for 54 bees recovered and flew back to the hive, "where they probably informed their companions of such an adventure and escape."

Rats, larger than mice, might not be able to enter a hive, but they still posed a threat to colonists, particularly their stores. The bees' sweet honey was part of a rather grim solution suggested in the local newspaper:

> *May 15. A never-failing remedy, to destroy rats out of any house, warehouse, ships, &c. Take sponge, and after having cut it into small pieces, as much as a rat can swallow, soak it in melted honey; put these pieces in plates near their holes, and a few experiments will shew the superior effect of this simple method to that of any of the numerous pretenders who call themselves rat catchers.*
> —Virginia Gazette, *July 15, 1773*

Wax moths, also called bee moths, were a serious trouble, coming into the hive to lay their eggs, which, when hatched as larvae, spun webs to take over the hives and force the bees to leave. The best defense against the moth seemed to be regular inspection, as suggested by eighteenth-century London bee man (and author and showman) Thomas Wildman.

Trouble in the hive might come from other honeybees. European black bees, the kind the British brought to America, are not known for being passive. They swarm readily and fight with rival hives, sometimes entering others' hives to steal honey.

Apiculture may also have been slow to grow due to an epidemic of American foulbrood disease (AFB), which is still very much a problem today. In AFB, bacterial spores form on the bees' larvae, and infected brood die before they can hatch. Although adult bees cannot die from AFB, they can carry the spores into the hive, where it will ultimately weaken and likely destroy the colony. Shared equipment between infected and previously unaffected hives can also spread the disease. The only known treatments are irradiating the hive, obviously not available to colonial farmers, and deliberately destroying the hive to prevent any further chance of spread. European foulbrood also exists; though more common, it is more easily treatable and does not produce persistent spores.

By the mid-nineteenth century, modest farmers, such as Southampton County resident Lemuel Story (?–1845) and later his son Elliott (1821–1886), might have owned several hundred acres, but all the land wasn't necessarily productive. In the Storys' case, as recounted in an article by G. Herndon in *Agricultural History* based on family diaries, much of it was swampland. They kept bees to provide honey for their own table, and, if they ran short, they might supplement with wild honey found in the wilder areas of the property, though those bee trees sometimes "contained only old comb and no honey." They managed to be self-sufficient, clothing and feeding the family and keeping no slaves, although Elliott did have two hired hands, one Black and one white. Elliott tried to supplement his small farming income with side jobs. He briefly became a merchant with the firm Edwards & Story of Franklin, Virginia. He also taught at the Blackwater Free School and eventually served as justice of the peace in Southampton County.

ON PLANTATIONS

On plantations, as opposed to family farms, the majority of hands-on work would be done by enslaved people. Landon Carter, of Sabine Hall in Lancaster County, left behind a diary chronicling both his public and plantation life in the eighteenth century, from 1752 to 1778. Carter was sent to England for a classical education as a young man. Upon his return, he was expected to take his place in his society, which included running the plantation and holding public office. He noted that he lost many swarms in 1772 when his servants (enslaved workers) did not have clean hives ready for them.

With less daily work to do than small farmers, some plantation owners concentrated their time on leisure pursuits and hospitality. William Nivison Blow (1855–1907), in his book, *Tower Hill Before the Rebellion: A History of the Small Virginia Plantation*, laid out how an esteemed visitor's day might

Johnston, F.B., photographer. Sabine Hall, Richmond County, Virginia, 1932. *Carnegie Survey of the Architecture of the South, Library of Congress, Prints and Photographs Division.*

go. The plantation, built in 1746, still stands in Cape Charles, close to the Chesapeake Bay:

> He enters a long lane lined on each side by tall cedars, passes over a green lawn and his journey is done. He is then assisted to alight by his host, taken to the dining room, and refreshed by a mint julep, peach and honey, or hot apple toddy, according to the season. This ceremony being over, he is informed that he is in Liberty Hall where everything is at his disposal. He at first fears that time will drag, but soon finds his apprehensions are groundless. There is an excellent library, and even in the beautiful days that are so common in this climate, one is tempted to remain indoors to examine it. The old leather bindings hint at something curious, while other shelves are filled with modern works, and tables are strewn with magazines and newspapers—a week or two old it is true—but he soon becomes accustomed to being a little behind the times.
>
> After examining the library and mapping amusement for more than one rainy day, and having enjoyed the curiously built house with its primitive furniture, the guest—if he is the right sort of man—is ready for the more serious sports of the chase. He must make his selection now, for if it is Autumn, nearly every kind of hunting is in season. The program is usually deer hunting in the forenoon; a mint julep, dinner, pipe, book and a nap; and quail or squirrel hunting in the afternoon.

The hostess's tasks to provide for guests went beyond the chase and the library, as "the rations for the entire farm were issued under her supervision and the making of cloth and clothing under her direction." She supervised and sewed along with the enslaved seamstresses who made clothing, inspected poultry, made preserves and strained honey, while also tending the sick. The fruits of these labors were realized throughout the house and on the table, as Blow writes:

> *The Virginia idea of living was generous too in those days; more meats, vegetables and breads than are commonly seen not at a meal were thought necessary—For Breakfast the family would sit down to egg-bread, hot rolls, beaten (sometimes called Maryland) biscuits, eggs, possibly a meat and a relish, and honey and coffee.*

After the Civil War, books came out that looked back on plantation life from the point of view of the planters' families, including the one quoted here. Martha McCulloch-Williams's *Dishes & Beverages of the Old South* weaves some of what she remembered into a narrative, and a portion of that has to do with beeswax:

> *Cakes of beeswax were kept in the Jackson press, so children, white and black, could not take bites for chewing. It ranked next to native sweet gum for such uses—but Mammy felt it had much better be saved to mix with the tallow at melting time. It made the candles much firmer, also bettered their light, and moreover changed the tallow hue to an agreeable very pale yellow. Bee hives, like much else, were to a degree primitive—the wax came from comb crushed in the straining of honey. It was boiled in water to take away the remnant sweetness, then allowed to cool on top of the water, taken off, and remelted over clean water, so manipulated as to free it from foreign substances, then molded into cakes. One cake was always set apart for the neighborhood cobbler, who melted it with tallow and rosin to make shoemaker's wax. Another moiety was turned into grafting wax—by help of it one orchard tree bore twelve manners of fruit. And still another, a small, pretty cake from a scalloped patty pan, found place in the family work basket—in sewing by hand with flax thread, unless you waxed it, it lost strength, and quickly pulled to pieces.*

Martha (Collins) McCulloch-Williams (1857–1934) was raised on a plantation in Tennessee. She eventually moved to New York City, where she married and had a successful literary career. Although garnished with outdated—and frankly insulting—language and ideas, the information from her book on how things were done is useful to those who study history. The uncomplicated way to render beeswax and its many handy uses were much the same, whether on vast plantations or more modest farms.

Agricultural Societies and Fairs

This lifestyle of leisure for the planters, so different from what was experienced by the small farmer and his own laborers, very much followed the pattern of the English gentlemen from whom many were descended. The Virginia planters, like their distant English relations, got caught up in the mid-1700s to 1800s Agricultural Revolution with its scientific and mechanical breakthroughs. More extensive crop rotations enriched the soil. Selective breeding for desirable livestock characteristics became more normal, and the inventions of mechanical farm machinery—including the McCormick Reaper, which was invented in Virginia—made farmwork less labor intensive.

Local agricultural fairs, sponsored by local farmers' societies, were (and

The Southern Planter 20, no. 7 (July 1860). Richmond: McFarlane & Fergusson. *Biodiversity Heritage Library.*

remain) popular, both as ways to show off farm products and equipment and as much-anticipated social events that might include horse-racing and dances.

An advertisement for the Fairfax Agricultural Fair and Cattle Show in 1852 listed many contest categories, including a premium (prize) of one dollar for the best five pounds of honey that had been taken from the hive without harming the bees.

In 1811, several planters meeting in Richmond formed the Virginia Society for Promoting Agriculture, with the idea of making farming of the same importance as commerce and manufacturing. At the following year's meeting, James M. Garnett of Fredericksburg suggested that agricultural tours be done throughout the state, like those popular in western Europe, to see what agricultural reforms could be found and later promoted.

This group faded after some years, but in 1820, the first state society was reorganized at a meeting at Parker's Tavern at Cabin Point in Surry County and was renamed the United Agricultural Society of Virginia. John James Parker's tavern was a convenient inn and stagecoach stop, along the Old Stage Road from Suffolk to Petersburg. They hoped to serve as a clearinghouse for local agricultural societies who wanted to voice their objections to tariffs on farming being proposed in Washington, D.C.

The group went through several more iterations and name changes, ultimately holding the first regular state fair in Richmond in November 1853, although there had been some statewide fairs also in the 1840s. The 1853 event had Richmond chipping in for the costs, and the railroad provided convenient transportation. Virginia farmers supported two long-standing publications that promoted the fair, Edmund Ruffin's *Farmer's Register* and G.F. Ruffin's *Southern Planter*. Planters also wrote for and subscribed to other farming journals from around the nation, in which inventive new ways of doing the old work of farming were shared. The state society continued to meet, and newly elected society president Willoughby Newton praised the McCormick reaper and stressed the need for more scientific farming. The group sent out a brochure to farmers across the state:

> *Come from the East and from the West, from the North and from the South of our glorious Old Dominion. Come with your wives and your daughters, come with your horses, with your cattle, and your sheep, and with your swine, with your implements of agriculture and with the products of your soil, and come up one mighty host of farmers inspired by the progressive spirit of the age. Come prepared to show what the agriculture of our state is now and what you design it to be in the future in which sloth will be a crime, mediocrity a reproach and ignorance a disgrace.*

Swirling around the agricultural society's reinvention was an increasingly pressing debate on slavery, but there was little to no talk of its abolishment among the planters, only high-sounding yet ridiculous justifications. The institution was not invisible. An enslaved man named Randolph received a prize for the best ploughing shown on the grounds at the first state fair.

The next year, the society president announced the fair to be a success. Now, he wanted to draw the society's attention to agricultural education, for the farmer

> *is left entirely without education, or with such defective, partial learning as to be acquired in schools which ignore the whole subject of theory and*

practice of agriculture as completely as if all science and all learning had no application, to or no connection with, and no uses in the most universal, the most necessary, the most complete and the most difficult of human occupations.

His solution: start a school or department of agriculture at a university, such as the University of Virginia or the Virginia Military Institute, but those plans did not come to fruition.

The state fairs continued, with horse races being a big draw. In 1857, Petersburg became the host city, and 1858 saw record crowds. The last fair before the Civil War took place in Richmond, October 22–27, 1860. All sorts of inventions were exhibited, prizes were given to essays on farm management and there was talk of beginning a separate state agricultural college. Plans for that were put on hold until well after the bloody conflict that was soon to commence.

Some time after the war, fairs began again, and local papers ran the news when local farmers did well in competition:

MR. KOEPPEN'S PRIZES AT STATE FAIR

Mr. Chas. Koeppen, of this city (Fredericksburg), won prizes at the State Fair as follows: Three firsts on comb and extracted honey. Two firsts and 2 seconds on bees. One first and one second on two entries of beeswax. First on collection of farm products for Spotsylvania county, amounting in the aggregate to $135. Mr. Koeppen also sold a quantity of his honey.
—Free Lance, *October 16, 1909*

Mr. Koeppen had ambition and advertised his bees for sale nationally in the January 1906 issue of *The Beekeepers' Review*: "Superior Stock: I make a specialty of Long-Tongue Italian, Carniolan, and Caucasian."

All are subspecies of the European honeybee. The Carniolans, native to Slovenia and its environs (Carniola being the old name for Slovenia— once part of the Roman Empire and later part of the Austro-Hungarian Empire) were known for being gentle but also able to defend themselves against pests. While Caucasian bees are gentle to work with, they use a lot of propolis for strengthening their hives, which can make them hard for a keeper to manage. Their outstanding characteristic is their exceedingly long tongues, which allow them to collect nectar from flowers other honeybees cannot manage. They also are most active in collecting in the summer, so they might not be a good choice for areas where the "flow" of nectar-producing plants happens mainly in early spring. Italian bees are beloved by many keepers for their sweet temperaments, although they tend to not do as well in cold climates.

Mr. Koeppen was not selling the feisty British black bee, also known as European dark bee—the kind brought to Jamestown. In the early part of the twentieth century, the black bees, so adaptable to wet and cold climates, were nearly killed off in their native Britain by Isle of Wight Disease (*Nosema apis*), also known as Acarine, a mite infestation that attacks the bees' tracheas.

BEE KIND—AND WEALTHY!

The careful treatment of bees—for everyone's benefit—is an ages-old idea. As noted in an earlier chapter, farmer-poet Tusser gave these Renaissance-era recommendations for helping the bees:

Place hive in good ayer, set southly and warme,
and take in due season wax, honie, and swarme.
Set hive on a plank, (not too low by the ground)
where herbe with flowers may compass it round:
And boards to defend it from north and north east,
from showers and rubbish, from vermin and beast.

Go look to thy bees, if the hive be too light,
set water and honie, with rosemary dight.
Which set in a dish full of sticks in the hive
from danger of famine yee save them alive.

Take heede to thy bees, that are readie to swarme,
the losse thereof now is a crownes worth of harme.
Let skilfull be readie and diligence seene,
least being too careles, thou losest thy bees.

The Redoubtable Mr. Wildman

Robbing the bees without necessarily murdering them was an advancement to which early American beekeepers aspired. The showmanship of eighteenth-century British beekeeper Thomas Wildman (1734–1781) popularized the notion with his newsworthy demonstrations of apiary harmony that were reprinted in colonial newspapers.

The following appeared on the front page of the *Virginia Gazette* of December 11, 1766:

(London)

Sept. 15. Conversation turns much on the uncommon skill of Mr. Wildman, in the taming and managing of bees, Mr. Wildman, armed with his friendly bees, thinks himself indefensible against the fiercest mastiffs, and actually did at Salisbury encounter three yard dogs, one after the other.

The conditions of engagement were, that he should have notice of the dog being set at him. Accordingly the first mastiff was set loose, and as he approached two bees were detached, who stung him, the one on the nose, the other on the flank; upon receiving the wounds, the dog retired very much daunted. After this the second dog entered the lists and was foiled with the same expedition as the first. The third dog was at last brought against the champion, but the animal, observing the ill success of his brethren, would not attempt to sustain a combat, so retired with his tail on his back.

But Mr. Wilder's (and his bees') deeds were not yet done. On the second page of the same issue:

We have received the following account of Mr. Wildman's performances, at the Earl Spencer's seat at Wimbledon, Surry. The first of his performances was with one hive of bees hanging on his hat, which he carried in his hand, and the hive which they came out of in the other hand; which was to convince the Earl and Countess that he could take honey and wax without destroying the bees. Then he returned into the room and came out again with them hanging on his chin, as a very venerable beard. After showing them to the company, he took them out upon the grass walk facing his Lordship's window, where a table and tablecloth were immediately brought out, and he set the hive upon the table, and made the bees hive therein; then he made the bees come out again and swarm in the air, the Ladies and Nobility standing amongst them, and no person stung by them; he made them go on the table,

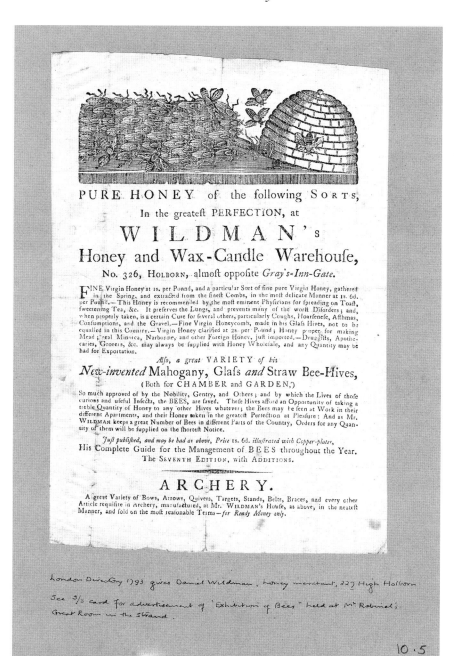

PURE HONEY of the following SORTS,

In the greateſt PERFECTION, at

WILDMAN's

Honey and Wax-Candle Warehouſe,

No. 326, HOLBORN, almoſt oppoſite *Gray's-Inn-Gate*.

FINE Virgin Honey at 1s. per Pound, and a particular Sort of fine pure Virgin Honey, gathered in the Spring, and extracted from the fineſt Combs, in the moſt delicate Manner at 1s. 6d. per Pound.—This Honey is recommended by the moſt eminent Phyſicians for ſpreading on Toaſt, ſweetening Tea, &c. It preſerves the Lungs, and prevents many of the worſt Diſorders; and, when properly taken, is a certain Cure for ſeveral others, particularly Coughs, Hoarſeneſe, Aſthmas, Conſumptions, and the Gravel.—Fine Virgin Honeycomb, made in his Glaſs Hives, not to be equalled in this Country.—Virgin Honey clarified at 2s. per Pound; Honey proper for making Mead; real Minorca, Narbonne, and other Foreign Honey, juſt imported.—Druggiſts, Apothecaries, Grocers, &c. may always be ſupplied with Honey Wholeſale, and any Quantity may be had for Exportation.

Alſo, a great VARIETY *of his*

New-invented Mahogany, Glaſs *and* Straw Bee-Hives,

(Both for CHAMBER and GARDEN,)

So much approved of by the Nobility, Gentry, and Others; and by which the Lives of thoſe curious and uſeful Inſects, the BEES, are ſaved. Theſe Hives afford an Opportunity of taking a treble Quantity of Honey to any other Hives whatever; the Bees may be ſeen at Work in their different Apartments, and their Honey taken in the greateſt Perfection at Pleaſure: And as Mr. WILDMAN keeps a great Number of Bees in different Parts of the Country, Orders for any Quantity of them will be ſupplied on the ſhorteſt Notice.

Juſt publiſhed, and may be had at above, Price 1s. 6d. *illuſtrated with Copper-plates,*

His Complete Guide for the Management of BEES throughout the Year.

The SEVENTH EDITION, with ADDITIONS.

ARCHERY.

A great Variety of Bows, Arrows, Quivers, Targets, Stands, Belts, Braces, and every other Article requiſite in Archery, manufactured, at Mr. WILDMAN's Houſe, as above, in the neateſt Manner, and ſold on the moſt reaſonable Terms—*for Ready Money only.*

London Directory 1793 gives Daniel Wildman, honey merchant, 327 High Holborn

See 3/5 card for advertisement of "Exhibition of Bees" held at Mr. Robinet's Great Room in the Strand.

10·5

Wildman, T. *A Treatise on the Management of Bees*, London, 1768. *Public domain.*

and took them up by handfuls and tossed them up and down like so many pease; then made them go into their hive at the word of command.

At 5 o'clock in the afternoon he exhibited again with the three swarms of bees, one on his head, one on his breast, and the other on his arm, and then went into his Lordship, who was too much indisposed to see the former experiments; the hives which the bees were taken from were carried by one of the servants. He went into a room again, and came out with them all over his head, face, and eyes, and was led blind before his Lordship's window. He then begged of his Lordship that he would lend him one of his horses, which was granted, and was brought out in his body clothes. He then mounted the horse, with the bees all over his head and face (except his eyes) and breast, and left arm, with a whip in his right hand, and the groom then led the horse backwards and forwards by his Lordship's window for some time. He then took the reins in his hand and rode around the house. He then dismounted, and made the bees march upon a table, and commanded them to retire to their hives; which they accordingly did, and gave great satisfaction to the Earl, the Countess, and all the spectators.

Not every performance went as smoothly, however:

Mr. Wildman having been informed that it has been reported that in his exhibitions of his command over bees, at Marybone Gardens, the bees stung several persons who were his spectators, declares that this report is absolutely false, no one having been stung but himself by one bee, and that owing to his own imprudence. It having been industriously spread likewise that his command over bees is a matter of mere curiosity, and of no use, he begs leave to assure the publick that by his method of getting the bees from the hive when he pleases, and taking their wax and honey, he can from the same stock get half as much more than is now taken in the common method.
—Virginia Gazette, *January 15, 1767*

Thomas Wildman, whose unusual skeps opened at the top and had removable bars for easier access, had his fans among the Americans, too. Benjamin Franklin, ever a curious man, was a patron for his 1768 *Treatise on the Management of Bees.* Franklin had a particular interest in bees. As noted in Deborah Jean Warner's *Sweet Stuff: An American History of Sweeteners, from Sugar to Sucralose*, he made strong arguments that Americans should be more careful beekeepers so that they might free themselves from the cost and unhealthiness of imported sugar and molasses.

According to Pryor, agricultural authors had begun advocating for box hives by the late colonial period. These hives were stackable, with a pathway for the bees between them. When one box was filled with honey, another could be added to give them more space. With multiple entrances/exits, the bees could retreat into another part of their hives while their honey was being taken. In 1817, the *Lynchburg Press* reprinted an article from a New Jersey paper discussing a kind of box that allowed honeybees to be taken without being killed. In 1818, a similar article ran in the *Genius of Liberty*, which found its way to desk of Thomas Jefferson at Monticello.

To Market!

In 1729, Governor William Gooch was asked about the natural produce of Virginia by the Board of Trade in London. He replied that beeswax was one of the colonies' natural products of value. According to Governor Gooch's report, almost every ship sailing from Virginia to the West Indies or Portugal/Spain carried with it a supply of beeswax. The beeswax was used in connection with the making of wine barrels and other containers in those countries, as mentioned in the Spring 2018 issue of the *Journal of the Eastern Apicultural Society of North America*, which held its conference in Virginia that year.

The total amount of beeswax exported from Virginia in 1730 (just over one hundred years since the first import of honeybees to North America) was 156 quintals, equal to 156,000 kilograms, or about 343,900 pounds, according to Pryor. Ships bound for Barbados in the late colonial period might list a keg of honey among their exports, and beeswax was frequently shipped to foreign shores, according to Pryor.

In May 1805, Richmond merchants Gamble & Son listed the many goods they were ready to trade: Madeira, West Indian rum, sugar, pepper, scythes, whetstones, snuff, brown Hessians (boots) and more. They sought goods from locals to export, giving "the highest rates…for Bees-Wax, good Bear, Deer, and Otter Skins, and other shipping Furr," as advertised in the *Virginia Argus*, July 31, 1805.

Decades later, with the railroad and its handy depots to aid in shipping, merchants such as William Menzel and Son in New York were eager to get their warehouses filled with Virginia's "Ginseng, Feathers, Beeswax, Dried Fruit, Furs, Sineca Root, Metals, Rags, flaxseed, &c., &c., &c., &c," according to the *Bristol News*, April 7, 1874.

"L.L. Langstroth at Age 80."
From *Langstroth on the Hive &*
Honey Bee, rev. by Dadant.
Biodiversity Heritage Library.

There were plenty of hive goods to ship, and that would increase with the invention of the Langstroth hive in the 1850s, which made beekeeping profitable on a larger scale. Reverend Lorenzo Langstroth (1810–1895), an American Congregational minister, took the idea of a hive with moveable pieces one step further. He discovered and promoted "bee space"—that is, that the perfect space between combs would allow them to be easily removed, making honey production easier and more profitable. He discovered that if the distance between combs was too small, worker bees would fill it with sticky propolis to seal up the gap. If it were too wide, they would try to make another comb. Either scenario made it hard and dangerous to remove the comb from the protective bees. The concept of bee space had been known in Europe since the 1840s, but Langstroth used his own calculations in his top-opening, moveable frame hive, patented in 1852.

Merchants advertised their honey stock in local newspapers. Edward O. Ralls & Company had advertised via the *Richmond Whig* in 1845 that its clarified honey could be had "for sale low" at an old stand on Main Street. "FRESH HONEY, in the comb" was another option listed in the *Alexandria Gazette* by James E. McGraw, also in 1845. For those wanting more than a small supply, gallons of honey could be had from druggists for hotels and restaurants, as advertised by P. Johnston & Bro. in a December 1860 issue of the *Daily Dispatch*.

"TELLING THE BEES" AND MORE BEE LORE

Honeybees' mysterious yet often observable ways and their proximity to humans conjured a number of folk beliefs. One of the most eerie yet lovely is the need to tell the bees of any great change in the family's circumstances—marriage, birth, but especially death, lest the bees feel slighted at not knowing that their keeper has passed. It was the custom to drape the hives in black crepe for mourning, as the bees would share the family's sadness. Not remembering this courtesy could lead to their flight.

American poet John Greenleaf Whittier (1807–1892) captures the melancholy custom of telling the bees of the death of their beekeeper in a poem. Here is a portion:

> *Before them, under the garden wall,*
> *   Forward and back,*
> *Went drearily singing the chore-girl small,*
> *   Draping each hive with a shred of black.*
> *Trembling, I listened: the summer sun*
> *   Had the chill of snow;*
> *For I knew she was telling the bees of one*
> *   Gone on the journey we all must go!*

"A cottager leaned whispering by her hives, telling the bees some news, as they lit down, and entered one by one their waxen town." From *The Monitions of the Unseen, and Poems of Love and Childhood* by Jean Ingelow, 1871. *Library of Congress.*

her loyal subjects assemble around her, and form a living cluster. Quickly, from all sides, they continue to gather, and in a quarter of an hour or twenty minutes a dense mass will be hanging one to the other, till it seems wonderful the queen and those in the interior of the living ball are not suffocated.

FIG. 61.—"TANGING."

In country places it is still the custom to beat warming-pans, tin kettles, frying-pans, or other unmusical vessels, with keys or sticks or hammers, while the bees are swarming, under the idea that the noise makes them settle the more quickly. That any

"Tanging" from *The Honey-bee; Its Nature, Homes and Products*, W.H. Harris. *Biodiversity Heritage Library.*

There is lore surrounding capturing bee swarms, too. As Elizabeth Pryor relates in her report, an author suggested putting twigs of fennel or balm in nearby bushes to draw the bees to settle, while others covered a new hive with pleasant herbs and sugar water to welcome them.

And, as mentioned earlier, tanging or beating metal objects together was believed to force bees to land rather than fly away. Another author suggested firing a pistol, charged with powder, between the bees and the hive so they would settle on the first bush they could.

Some English customs concerning bees that would have been brought over by immigrants were gathered in W. Hand's article "Anglo-American Folk Belief and Custom: The Old World's Legacy to the New."

Hand remarks that bees had a special place in folklore because they were thought to have almost human qualities and sensitivity. For example, in some parts of England, including Herefordshire, it was believed that bees will not thrive in a quarrelsome family, as they are lovers of peace—and have an aversion to noise. Others contend that quarrels concerning the bees themselves will keep them from prospering.

There were other beliefs that bees could not abide swearing or "unchastity"—possibly a variation of the belief that beekeepers needed to be scrupulously clean before attending to the hive. In some parts of England, it was thought that a virgin could walk through a swarm without being stung. Hand, the author, could find no similar belief in America.

Beyond the importance of telling the bees about a death in the family as a courtesy, others regarded bees as sometimes being portents of death themselves, such as a swarm visible on a pile of dead wood.

Now, how one tells the bees varied, using a loud voice in New Hampshire or whispering in Kentucky. In Hampshire, England, according to Thiselton Dyer, there was a formal verse to say:

Bees, bees, awake!
Your master is dead,
And another you must take.

Other parts of England had the beekeeper's widow knocking on the hives, crying, "He's gone! He's gone!" The bees' humming reply was their promise to stay.

Besides talking to the bees, the bereaved might let them know by turning or moving the hives, tapping them with the house key or draping them with black crepe. In England, the winged ones sometimes received a bit of wine, funeral biscuit (cookies) and the like. Bees were also privy to happy news, such as weddings. Speaking of weddings, dreaming of bees or a girl finding one in her shoe was a wedding portent.

As bees were rather more highly regarded than working beasts, it isn't surprising that there were certain rules about acquiring them. In older times in England, you purchased bees with gold. In North Carolina, there was a custom to never receive payment for a beehive in the hand, lest one sell his luck. Instead, the buyer would lay silver coins on a rock, which the seller would pick up once the bees were in his possession.

In Maryland and Kentucky, having bees swarm on February 22 or May 1 was considered most fortunate. Tanging, as previously mentioned, was known in England to get bees to settle, but in America, the musicians added

Left: Using a skep to gather a hive. *From* Die Gartenlaube, *1897.*

Right: A widow and her son telling the bees of a death in the family. Detail of "The Widow," by Charles Napier Hemy, 1895. *Public domain.*

in ringing bells. This rhyme is known in both Dorset, England, and New York, with many regional variations:

A swarm of bees in May
Is worth a load of hay;
A swarm of bees in June
Is worth a silver spoon;
A swarm of bees in July
Is not worth a fly.

In the Bee Tree

Wild bees were a force of nature that often figured in countryside stories. An article on folklore of Elizabeth City County, Virginia, included African American folklore collected at the Hampton Institute about 1900. The Brer (Brother) Rabbit stories, of which this is one, are an especially rich vein of trickster tales:

Brer Buzzard was going to kill Brer Rabbit. One day Brer Buzzard met Brer Rabbit in the road. Brer Rabbit had two jugs of syrup. Brer Buzzard said, "If you don't give me one of those jugs, I will kill you." He gave one of them to Brer Buzzard. Then Brer Buzzard said, "You will have to give me both jugs." Brer Rabbit did so. "Now I have both jugs," said Brer Buzzard, "and I am going to kill you, anyhow." Brer Rabbit said, "Brer Buzzard, please let me off, and I will carry you to a bee-tree." Brer Buzzard said, "All right!" They went on; and when they got to the tree, Brer Rabbit went up first and ate honey until he saw the bees and came down.

Then Brer Buzzard went up. He was so greedy, that the bees stung him on the head. It swelled in the hollow so that he could not get it out. Then Brer Buzzard said to Brer Rabbit, "Run for the doctor, and ask him what I shall do!" Brer Rabbit ran around the tree, and said, "Two good wrings and one good snatch." But that wouldn't do. Brer Rabbit ran around the tree again, and said, "Take the hatchet and chop it out." Brer Buzzard said, "Come on, and get it out for me!" Brer Rabbit went up there and chopped around, and then cut his head off. Then Brer Rabbit got a piece of mud and put it on his neck, and said, "Now flutter, now flutter, if you can!"

The Beehive in the Ghost Tree

Sometimes bees were only incidental to an often-told folktale, with the meat of it centering on something much more serious. As late as 1994, the *Rappahannock Record* reported on the Ghost Tree of Ottoman, a community "nestled on a peninsula between the Rappahannock River and the Western Branch of the Corrotoman." Blown down in the months before the story was written, its huge trunk "as big as three trees in any abandoned hedgerow or fencerow" revealed an equally large beehive.

The giant poplar stood along Route 354, just north of the Route 692 intersection. Its history stretched back centuries. The property owner, a Mr. Ficklin, theorized that it was the survivor of a row of poplar trees that helped people find their way from the Rappahannock to the Potomac River. Lifelong resident Captain Tom Stevens said it had been called the Ghost Tree or the Hanging Tree, having been used for that purpose in the 1800s or earlier. Older residents said it was a place where enslaved people were whipped and hanged. At night, the elderly people told the grandchildren, their ghosts came out to the tree.

Newspaper columns on bees often included choice bits of folklore. A sidebar on Dr. Clendening's nationally syndicated health column in the 1940s relates the belief that if a honeybee lights on the lips of a newborn, he will be eloquent, having the gift of sweet words, as was said of Saint Ambrose. Dr. Clendening himself was less impressed with honey's purported virtues, as it was said to be part of the favorite breakfast of a certain up-and-coming German dictator.

Nonetheless, the sweet golden stuff and its tiny makers fascinated readers, farmers and merchants alike. This chestnut appeared frequently in one form or another as column filler in local Virginia newspapers:

"How the Word Honeymoon Originated"

Among northern nations of Europe, in ancient times, it was the custom for newly married couples to drink metheglin or mead (a kind of wine made from honey) for thirty days after marriage. Antiquarians say that from this custom the term "honey month," or "honeymoon" originated. Whether or not that is its origin, it is known that in the days of marriage by capture the bridegroom remained in hiding with his bride until her kinsmen tired of the search for her. Later, when love entered marriage and elopements were frequent, the bride and bridegroom remained in hiding for

a while. Both of these "hiding periods" seem to point to possible origins of the honeymoon trip.
—*The* Highland Recorder *(Monterey, VA), February 4, 1938*

By the 1960s and 1970s, a number of colleges and universities realized the old ways were fast passing, as were the older people who knew about them. Folklore students were dispatched to glean what knowledge they could of past times before it was lost. Elmer L. Smith of Madison College strung a story for the December 21, 1967 issue of the *Recorder* on German American Christmas customs of the Shenandoah Valley that had been "handed down through the centuries."

Honey or Sugar Pot, Emanuel Suter (1833–1902) possibly at Dry River Pottery (active circa 1850–1890) Rockingham County, Virginia. Salt-glazed stoneware with cobalt decoration, circa 1850.
Collection of the Museum of the Shenandoah Valley, 2014.02.04.

One of the most popular practices he discovered was to have belsnicklers visiting homes during the holiday season. Smith and his professor John Stewart interviewed people who had belsnickled throughout the Valley, in eastern West Virginia and parts of Maryland. Who were the belsnicklers? Belsnickling visitors would arrive at their neighbors' homes on foot and be invited in for refreshments. The origins for belsnickling, Smith believed, were drawn from two German Yuletide characters: the Christ-Kindel and the Belsnickel. The Christ-Kindel rewarded the good children with gifts, and the Belsnickel punished the naughty ones. Young Smith's article also features the rather different Valley custom of Shanghiing, where Shangiers dressed in costume rode horseback or drove carriages or sleighs (the horses also decorated and disguised) in daylight. No hospitality was extended, but the Shangiers did make a lot of noise as they drove by!

Honey or Sugar Pot, Emanuel Suter (1833–1902). Reverse.
Collection of the Museum of the Shenandoah Valley, 2014.02.04.

By the late 1960s, only a few people were still belsnickling; it was mostly extinct. Shanghiing, which Smith and Stewart believed came from the celebration of St. Stephen's Day, had been popular in Pendleton County, West Virginia, as well as Highland and Augusta Counties in

Virginia, before World War I. But then it lost ground, what with automobiles becoming more popular than horses.

Now, as to bees, some folk whom the pair interviewed said that if you listen at a beehive at midnight on Christmas Eve, you can hear the bees singing, something that was also mentioned more detail in Hand's article on Anglo-American customs.

FOUNDING FATHERS
WERE BEEKEEPERS

As the colonies began their changeover to being an independent nation, they were very much an agricultural society. The new money being printed featured symbols of agriculture; a thirty-five-dollar bill for 1779 featured a plow in a field with the motto *Hinc opes*—"Hence our wealth." Philadelphia's Continental Congress put two skeps in a shelter on a forty-five-dollar bill, with the motto *Sic Floret Republica*—"Thus flourishes the Republic."

WASHINGTON AT MOUNT VERNON

To begin, George Washington was raised at Ferry Farm, just across the Rappahannock River from Fredericksburg. The eldest child of his father's second wife, Mary Ball, he eventually inherited Mount Vernon from his beloved half brother Lawrence, who died young. The future general and president kept a journal throughout his life, and, like many of the planters, he was interested in more modern ways of doing things. His library, which was largely sold off in the years following his death, contained *Lettres d'un Cultivateur Américain* (listed in the inventory as *Letters of American Farmer*, in French) by our bee-hunting friend de Crèvecoeur. Among Washington's other volumes on agriculture was *The Complete Farmer; or, A General Dictionary of Husbandry*, which has a section on bees and beekeeping.

The George Washington Pioneer Farmer site is a four-acre working farm near Mount Vernon that includes a re-creation of Washington's sixteen-sided treading barn. *Galen Parks Smith. (CC SA 3.0).*

Courtesy of the Mount Vernon Ladies' Association.

Skeps at Mount Vernon. *Courtesy of the Mount Vernon Ladies' Association.*

Washington also experimented with another form of sweetener, the honey locust tree. These native trees' pods were filled with a sweet paste. In October 1785, he noted in his diary, "Finding the Seeds of the Honey locust had come nearly, or quite to a state of maturity, although the thick part of the pod still retained its green colour, I had them gathered, lest when ripe they should be gathered by others to eat."

According to Washington's records, indentured English joiner Matthew Baldridge was issued several hundred nails from supplies "to make a bee house" in 1787. At some plantations, it was the custom for the planters to buy supplies from enslaved workers, who might keep their own chickens and beehives. Washington, who frequently had Indian (cornmeal) hoecakes with butter and honey for breakfast, sometimes bought his honey from Nat, a blacksmith; Davy, an overseer; and carpenters Sambo and Isaac—all of whom were enslaved.

Today, beekeepers using modern methods oversee hives that provide honey for Mount Vernon's gift shop.

Mercer and Mason

George Washington was a longtime friend of George Mason, whose stately home at Gunston Hall also has views of the Potomac River. That relationship went south when Mason, who would later be known as the "Father of the Bill of Rights," refused to sign the U.S. Constitution because he thought there were not enough guarantees of individual liberties and too much power was given to the government. His declaration of inalienable rights would go on to form the basis of the Bill of Rights, which was adopted by every state as a check on the Constitution.

As Mason was orphaned at a young age, his guardian was John Mercer, a planter at Marlborough Point in Stafford County. Mercer was a firebrand very much on the side of liberty. His library was large and justifiably renowned and included the aforementioned *Monarchy of the Bees*, as well as Trapp's *Virgil* in three volumes, translated into blank verse. According to *The Cultural History of Marlborough*, Mercer bought beeswax in some quantity from a farmer on the Eastern Shore, as well as bayberry wax, which could be mixed with beeswax for a pleasant-smelling light source for the young scholar.

Skeps in a stand, facing a garden. *Courtesy of the Mount Vernon Ladies' Association.*

JEFFERSON AT MONTICELLO

Thomas Jefferson spent his childhood at Tuckahoe Plantation, with his own family and the orphaned children of William Randolph, his mother's cousin. Jefferson had already begun studying classical languages and works by the time he was nine years old. At sixteen, he began two years at the College of William & Mary, graduating in 1762 with highest honors, having delved deeply into philosophy and mathematics, ready to take on legal studies under George Wythe.

Jefferson's later library at Monticello included dozens of volumes on agriculture, including those classic writers on things apian—Varro, Cato and Columella. He also owned Stephen White's *Collateral Bee-Boxes: Or, a New, Easy, and Advantageous Method of Managing Bees*. One of Jefferson's drawings of his estate shows poultry yards and bee houses, although he was also known to purchase quantities of beeswax. As was done at Mount Vernon, sometimes honey and other bee products were bought from the enslaved people on the plantation, in this case by Jefferson's granddaughter, Ann Cary Randolph, who served as housekeeper, who noted the purchases in her household accounts book.

Top: Johnston, F.B., photographer. Tuckahoe School House, Goochland County, Virginia, 1936. *Carnegie Survey of the Architecture of the South, Library of Congress, Prints and Photographs Division.*

Bottom: Johnston, F.B., photographer. Tuckahoe, Goochland County, Virginia, 1936. *Carnegie Survey of the Architecture of the South, Library of Congress, Prints and Photographs Division.*

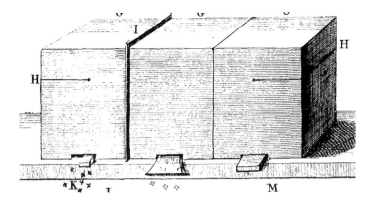

Collateral
Bee-boxes, or, a
New, Easy, and
Advantageous
Method of
Managing Bees.
Stephen White,
1759. *Fleuron:
A Database
of Eighteenth-
Century Printers'
Ornaments.*

Jefferson received this letter from a doctor—who was also a druggist, mayor, postmaster, banker, printer and, presumably, beekeeper—in the Shenandoah Valley, along with a container of honey:

From Solomon Henkel
New Market Shenandoah County Virginia July 5ᵗʰ 1817.
Respected Friend Thomas Jefferson

By Mr Thomas Tausy I Send you a glass tumbler full of Hony which I obtained from my Bees according to the Plan laid down by Mr Morgan of Prince Town of New Jersy. Finding the Methode so pleasing a one I thought it my duty to publish the Success I have had with it which I did as you will find in the gazette printed at Winchester accompaning this glass out of that publication you will find how I have managed the Boxes &c. Knowing you to be a Friend to all usefull improvements and Scients I have (by the request of Mr Tausy) taken the Liberty to Send you a present as above in hopes you will comunicate the Improvement to your Neighbours. (If you think it worthy of comunicating). Should you have discovered a better Plan then this or Some additional Improvements I would receive them with Pleasure as Some Gentlemen have requested me to have handbills Struck which will give a full account of the Management of Bees &c which I could have done at my printing office.

I remain your humble Servant
Solomon Henkel.

The gist of his attached article, reprinted in several newspapers, was how to take honey from hives without harming bees.

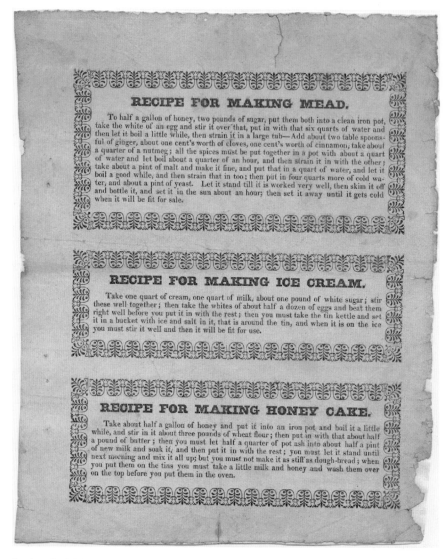

RECIPE FOR MAKING MEAD.

To half a gallon of honey, two pounds of sugar, put them both into a clean iron pot, take the white of an egg and stir it over that, put in with that six quarts of water and then let it boil a little while, then strain it in a large tub—Add about two table spoonsful of ginger, about one cent's worth of cloves, one cent's worth of cinnamon, take about a quarter of a nutmeg; all the spices must be put together in a pot with about a quart of water and let boil about a quarter of an hour, and then strain it in with the other; take about a pint of malt and make it fine, and put that in a quart of water, and let it boil a good while, and then strain that in too; then put in four quarts more of cold water, and about a pint of yeast. Let it stand till it is worked very well, then skim it off and bottle it, and set it in the sun about an hour; then set it away until it gets cold when it will be fit for sale.

RECIPE FOR MAKING ICE CREAM.

Take one quart of cream, one quart of milk, about one pound of white sugar; stir these well together; then take the whites of about half a dozen of eggs and beat them right well before you put it in with the rest; then you must take the tin kettle and set it in a bucket with ice and salt in it, that is around the tin, and when it is on the ice you must stir it well and then it will be fit for use.

RECIPE FOR MAKING HONEY CAKE.

Take about half a gallon of honey and put it into an iron pot and boil it a little while, and stir in it about three pounds of wheat flour; then put in with that about half a pound of butter; then you must let half a quarter of pot ash into about half a pint of new milk and soak it, and then put it in with the rest; you must let it stand until next morning and mix it all up; but you must not make it as stiff as dough-bread; when you put them on the tins you must take a little milk and honey and wash them over on the top before you put them in the oven.

Recipes for Making Mead, Ice Cream and Honey Cake, nineteenth century. Attributed to the Henkel family of New Market, Virginia. *Originally part of the Henry Tusing Collection. Courtesy of the Library of Virginia.*

At Stratford Hall

Monticello, located in the Virginia piedmont, or foothills, is quite a colonial distance from the Lee family's impressive home of Stratford Hall in Westmoreland County. Now a historic site that may be visited most days, Stratford was built under the auspices of Thomas Lee (1690–1750) on the site of The Clifts plantation that overlooks the Potomac River. Two of his sons, Richard Henry Lee and Francis Lightfoot Lee, signed the Declaration of Independence, a document framed by Jefferson. Stratford would later be owned by Henry "Light Horse Harry" Lee, a hero of the American Revolution. It was also the birthplace of his youngest son, Robert, who lived there for not quite four years before the property was sold because of his family's debts.

There is a note in Richard Henry Lee's memorandum book from August 3, 1782, that reads: "pd Ben[jamin] Weaver for 2 Gals of honey with an order for 3 barls [barrels] corn at 8/ pr barrel." Ben Weaver was also a Westmoreland County resident, possibly an overseer at Wakefield—George Washington's birthplace. County records for 1782 show that Benjamin Weaver held five enslaved persons.

In a later note on June 9, 1784, Richard Henry Lee set down a recipe for a honey-enriched throat gargle:

> *Where a salivation is to be removed wash the mouth with the follow Gargle ½ ounce Gum Arabic dissolved in half pint of boiling water add one ounce of honey of roses and drink freely of this ptisan* [tisane] *Barley wat*[er] *2 pints 2 ounces gum Arabic & 2 drams pure nitre with 1 ounce W. sugar—& purge—"*

In 2011, Stratford Hall initiated a partnership with a producer of all-natural honey, allowing its Cliff Fields to be used as the bees' home base. Their several thousand pounds of honey were sold both at the museum's shop and at retailers throughout the state. Stratford Hall has also hosted beekeeping lectures and workshops, taught by the Northern Neck Beekeepers Association.

One of President James Monroe's homes in the piedmont, Highland, has been opened to the public, and it has elected to make honeybees an important part of the site. Highland has hosted mead and honey tasting events, as well as the Albemarle County Fair, where the Central Virginia Beekeepers Association displayed an observation hive. Working in tandem with Thomas

Left: Beehive Honey Pot, Paul Storr, British, 1798–99, silver, Huntington Museum of Art. *Image by Daderot; public domain.*

Right: Albarello drug jar used for Simple Honey of Roses, Italy. *Science Museum, London. Attribution 4.0 International (CC BY 4.0).*

A three-hundred-year-old white oak tree and the house at James Monroe's Highland farm, Charlottesville Virginia. *Photo by Rain0975. CC BY-ND 2.0*

James Monroe's Highland farm, Charlottesville, Virginia. *Photo by Rain0975. CC BY-ND 2.0*

Jefferson's Monticello, as well as Tufton, another of Jefferson's properties, beekeepers Paul Legrand and Leslie Bouterie see establishing hives as a form of "ecological stewardship." Plans are underway to interpret the hives in their visitor areas. As of now, the bees provide excellent pollination for the historic gardens, and raw honey, foraged from nectar in Monticello gardens and farms, can be found for sale at its gift shop. The carefully tended bees at Tufton are the Russian variety—a mix of Italian and Carniolan—that has some natural resistance to bee mites.

Looking back to the Revolutionary War, where many of these planters served as leaders, embargoes on British goods, including molasses and sugar mainly coming from the Caribbean, were a predictable consequence. Homegrown honey of North America's fields and forests, as well as maple syrup when it could be had, sweetened those difficult times, as it would do in a century and a bit later during the world wars.

A Growing Body of Knowledge

After the Revolution, wealthy men and scholarly sorts were no longer the only ones to keep collections of books, particularly of a practical vein. More books and periodicals were being printed without the hindrance of a stamp tax, and the postal service, which operated in tandem with stagecoaches, made it possible to deliver printed materials throughout the states. There was a strong sense of national pride following America winning independence from Britain. Noah Webster devised a new American dictionary, which took in unusual words Americans would need to know. He also simplified spellings. Honey changed its flavour to flavor. British English was not in favour—American English was favored.

Between 1790 and 1820, Americans published a number of books on bee culture, and they weren't above filching a perfectly good tome, such as *A Short History of Bees*, which was originally printed in London in 1802 but could just as readily be sold from a Philadelphia press in 1803. Shorter books (pamphlets, really) such as T. Miner's *The Experienced Bee-Keeper* and J.A. Doddridge's *A Treatise on the Culture of Bees*, were put up for sale. In 1819, in Harrisburg, Pennsylvania, J.S. Wiestling published his *Die Vollstandige Bienen-Worter, oder Nützliche Anweisungen zur Bienen-Zucht* (roughly translated, *The Complete Bee Book, or Useful Instructions in Bee Cultivation*) for the still mainly German-speaking community that ranged down through Virginia's Shenandoah Valley and had access to newspapers written in their mother tongue. General books on agriculture might include lengthy sections on bee management, such as Butler's *The Farmer's Manual* (1819). It includes a treatise on bees that takes up 76 of its 224 pages.

Bees and their keepers made their presence known in local papers in antebellum Virginia. J.W. Johnson had bragging rights for his prize-winning honey at the fair in 1857, written up as it was in the *Weekly Advertiser*, which seemed to have a sweet spot for honey, as its editor received a golden gift from Edwin B. Allen in 1859. Merchants proudly advertised their supplies of fresh mountain honey, as did E.J. Picot, who sold it at the corner of Seventeenth and Main in Richmond on the eve of the war per the *Daily Dispatch*, September 9, 1859.

THE CIVIL WAR AND AFTER

In the days leading up to the Civil War, there were few hints of the food deprivation Virginians would soon face, particularly those who lived in cities. The city's bread riot in 1863 would certainly have been beyond their ken. The September 4, 1860 issue of Richmond's *Daily Dispatch* ran a proud advertisement:

> *COUNTRY PRODUCE; Fresh Mountain Butter; Bacon Hog-Round; Honey, in comb; Family Flour, in bags and barrels, &c.; receiving to-day, and for sale low, at J.P. KAVENAGH, 6th and Broad sts.*

By the following fall, families were making do. A wartime publication, the *Central Presbyterian*, gave these suggestions for using beeswax in its column for "The Planter and Housekeeper" in the October 26, 1861 issue:

> *A Valuable Salve.—The best ever used for man or beast. Linseed oil, two quarts; beeswax, three pounds; rosin, three pounds. Heat and stir the article until well-mixed.*
> *"Buffalo Robes"*
> *The growing scarcity of leather in the Confederate States will lead us to point out several plans of tanning hides and skins which are more expeditious than those generally practiced. Leather made by these new processes is apt to wet like a kid glove or buffalo robe, although it may wear well. Where little or no bark or tanooze* [an aqueous extract of tan-bark, such

as hemlock or oak bark] *of any kind is employed, the hide would be "stuffed" with tallow and beeswax to turn water. The skins of Buffalo are not even salted by the Indians on the Upper Missouri. They are beaten as they dry by women, to soften and expand the grain. No alum is used; and it is rather a misnomer to say they are tanned.*

Of course, honey has always been highly favored by soldiers living off others' farmsteads. As reported, or perhaps remembered, in Leesburg's newspaper *Genius of Liberty*, Lord Wellington gave a "Beehive Order" during the Spanish campaign against Napoleon:

Extract from a General Order issued by Lord Wellington, dated at Jariacejo, 16th August, 1809.

"The soldiers are again positively prohibited to plunder beehives. Any man found with a beehive in his possession will be punished."

This order did not deter the men from becoming "honey suckers," as will be seen by two subsequent orders dated at Badajos, Sept. 7th and 12th of the same year: "Soon after the first order on 'beehives' was issued at Jariacejo, Lord Wellington, in one of his rides, saw a man on the 88th or Connaught Rangers posting along as fast as his legs could carry him, with a beehive on his head. Lord W., furious at so flagrant a disobedience of orders, which sapped all discipline, called out to him, "Hillo! sir, where did you get that beehive?" Pat had enveloped his head and face in his great coat to prevent the bees stinging him, and thinking more of his prize than the tone of the voice addressed to him, answered in pure Milesian, "Jist over the hill, there; and by Jasus, if you don't make haste they'll be all gone."—The blind good-nature of Pat stayed the Duke's anger, and it was reported at dinner as a good joke. It was no joke afterwards, however, to the 4th division (of infantry,) as will be seen in the orders of the month following, when they got the name of "Honeysuckers," but they soon won for themselves another name in the field, and gained something sweeter than honey in a reputation which has buried the sobriquet in oblivion. The Connaught Rangers made part of the 4th division, which was, I believe, commanded by the brave Picton. —N.P.

There were "honeysuckers" (and unjustly accused honeysuckers) in America's Civil War, too.

John H. Worsham, one of "Stonewall" Jackson's Foot Cavalry, wrote a memoir, published approximately fifty years after the events described. He served in F Company of the Twenty-First Regiment Virginia Infantry. In October 1861, they found themselves in the mountains of the newly minted state of West Virginia:

We left Middle Mountain on the 28th, after a heavy rain. All the creeks had become small rivers, and as we forded them the water came up to our waists. We had now one two-horse and one three-horse wagon to move everything belonging to the command, and began to think, as Gen. Loring did, that we were men, but not soldiers. After a short march each day we reached Elk Mountain about dark on Oct. 1. A detail of a lieutenant and six men and a non-commissioned officer was made from F Company, and sent back eight miles on the road to picket.

We reached our destination about midnight. Two sentinels were posted at once, one in the road, the other in a path that led over the mountain, headquarters of the camp being at a spring on the road near a house, but on the opposite side of the road. The next morning, not long after day, the inmates of the house, a woman and her children, commenced to stir, and soon made their appearance. About sunrise the woman came to the yard fence, and commenced to abuse us in the most violent language I ever heard from a woman. It was some time before we could tell why she was abusing us.

She had quite a large number of beehives, and the troops marching by her house the day before molested none of them. When she arose in the morning, and knew that one of her best hives was gone, and a squad of men were at her spring, it was quite natural that she should think we took it. Our lieutenant, Edward Mayo, tried to impress on her that we did not; but she knew better, as she had gone to bed with everything all right, and when she awoke, we were there and the hive was gone. This was convincing proof to her. We were ordered not to go on her side of the road, nor have any talk with the inmates of the house, as Lieutenant Mayo would show her that we were gentlemen at any rate.

We had no rations, as we moved in the night, before we could get any. It is true that some of the men had a little sugar and coffee, and some a little raw meat and a few biscuit. After the old lady had cooled off, as we supposed, our lieutenant went over to the house and tried to borrow or hire a coffee pot, but the old lady said she would see him and us in a hot place sooner. On his return we built a small fire, boiled the meat, and divided the bread amongst us.

The woman now, to add to our misery, commenced to bring out her milk and carry it to the hog pen, pouring gallon after gallon to the hogs. We did not say a word to any of the household during the day. A little before night our lieutenant went over again to see what he could do, and with the offer of a little coffee, an article he found the old lady was very fond of and had been without for some time, he got the use of a teakettle to make some coffee in, and she baked us an oven of corn bread. He carried the articles back, and stayed in the porch, had quite a long chat, and returning, told us she promised to let us have the kettle and some more bread in the morning. In the morning we got them, with the promise of a dinner for the party. About dinner time we were relieved, and ordered to report back to camp. We waited for our dinner, and the old lady certainly did try herself. She gave us as nice a dinner as we ever had, including dessert, which made amends for the way in which she first treated us. She also apologized, and we left truly friends, and all kissed the baby.

There was no word on who might have taken the honey, the hive and the bees.

More than a year later, the Eighty-Seventh Regiment of the Pennsylvania Volunteers happened into a mountainous area now known as Blue Grass, Virginia. Located near the Devil's Backbone rock formation, a little over six miles north of Monterey, it runs along the South Branch of the Potomac River. During the Civil War—and up to 1950—it was known as Hightown or, more colloquially, Crab Bottom.

George Reeser Prowell, in his history of the Eighty-Seventh, found himself and his regiment in that district. Their intentions were not peaceful. Neither were the bees:

The weather was intensely cold. They did not want to leave that comfortable place, but in time of war orders must be obeyed. The mountain was crossed, and Col. Latham, with his two regiments, one battery, and ten wagons, arrived at Hightown, better known thought the surrounding country as "Crab Bottom," at 5 p.m. of that eventful Saturday, November 8, 1862, after completing one of the hardest and most romantic day's marches experienced by the regiment during the three years of its service.

The storm king came down upon them with unrelenting fury all day. It had snowed incessantly for two days and one night. It is doubtful whether the veterans of Valley Forge under Washington during the Revolution, endured the rigors of winter more heroically than did the hardy sons of Pennsylvania and West Virginia in this memorable campaign through the Alpine region of the Old Dominion....

Crab Bottom is at the head of a pretty little valley of the same name. The inhabitants, before the war, were a happy and contented people, who prospered fairly well in raising cattle and in cultivating their fields and gardens. Early in 1861, the doctrine of secession had been preached all through this region by emissaries from Richmond and the Shenandoah Valley. Most of the men in Crab Bottom had cast their lot with the Confederacy and had become the worst bushwhackers of the Civil War....

Col. Schall was requested to ask for forty volunteers from his regiment, who were to accompany a noted Union scout, by the name of Slaton and do whatever he demanded of them. The object of sending this party was to make a careful search throughout the valley, capture all bushwhackers they might come across and lay waste to their homes....

An enthusiastic forager was coming with a hive of bees. The weather had become warm that day, and the busy little bees wanted to know what kind of an excursion they were going on; so they found their way out of the hive and began to sting their captor in real earnest. He dropped the hive, and hastened into camp with a hundred bees following to pay their respects to him and his comrades.

Major Buehler looked up and said: "The boy didn't seem to know his gun was loaded. Wonder if he could run that fast if the Rebels were after him."

The majority of honeybees survived the foraging to forage themselves once more, as both bees and hives were advertised for sale in the *Fredericksburg Ledger* on the last day of January 1871. After the war, the men who survived it mainly went home, but some from the North, having seen opportunities in the burned-out lands, returned in civilian dress to start businesses and run farms. Some formerly enslaved people traveled north for a fresh start, starting new communities. But others elected to stay with their extended families.

In the 1870s, the artist Winslow Homer made a tour of Reconstruction-era Virginia and created paintings that were remarkable for their unusual subjects: African Americans, and specifically one young boy, who was the subject of several works—*Weaning the Calf, The Unruly Calf, A Flower for Teacher, Contraband* and *The Busy Bee*. All were painted in 1875 in the same rural setting. *The Busy Bee* shows the child on a day when the hive is humming. Homer's earlier works, particularly those drawn during wartime, had the crude, caricatured style popular in the magazines of the period, but these later paintings, showing a young freeborn generation, are exceptional for the moments in time they capture, as explained by Mary Ann Calo in the *American Art Journal*.

Left: From *History of the Corn Exchange Regiment, 118th Pennsylvania Volunteers, from their first engagement at Antietam to Appomattox…* U.S. Army Pennsylvania 118th Volunteers and John L. Smith, 1888. *Via Internet Archive Book Images.*

Right: *The Busy Bee* by Winslow Homer, 1875.

In the Appalachians, even as new kinds of hives and different types of bees were being tried elsewhere, bee gums and traditional bee varieties still sufficed for local needs:

> *"Untraveled Ways in Eastern Kentucky—Industrious Mountain Women"*
> *Correspondence of The Evening Star. Big Sandy, KY, May 1882.*

> *The honey bee is also a favorite. They are obtained from the woods in quantities to suit. Everybody hunts bees and domesticates as many swarms as desired. They are kept in hollow logs called beegums. These forests afford the finest pasturage for bees imaginable, and the beekeeping ought to be a great industry there. Rude as the externals are, there is comfort in most of these homes.*
> *The orchard is a constant attendant of the house. Peaches, apples, grapes, quinces, and all the small fruits are very fine. I did not see a single pear or cherry tree. We never sat down to a table which did not display honey, and at least three kinds of fruit, preserved or stewed.*
> —*The* Evening Star *(Washington, D.C.) May 27, 1882*

"Hiving the Bees." *From* Harper's Young People, *1879.*

SWEET SPIRITS AT MEADERIES

According to Sarah Hand Meacham's article in the *Virginia Magazine of History and Biography*, mead is a raw alcohol, only requiring honey and water (and yeast!), and before the latter half of the eighteenth century, making it was usually women's work, requiring little capital outlay. Meacham notes that making mead was frequently the woman's responsibility because she was likely the one keeping the bees, which provided honey for her cooking and were necessary to pollinate the garden. However, by the late seventeenth century, beekeeping had become more of a masculine pastime.

There are several types of mead:

TRADITIONAL MEADS. Made simply with honey, water and yeast. The honey varietals (and kinds of yeast used) are very much relied on for taste.

CYSERS. Meads made with apples. Virginia has a bounteous apple harvest, so cysers are popular here.

HYDROMEL. An old word for mead generally. These days, a mead that's classed as a hydromel has a lower alcohol content.

PYMENT. Meads made with grapes. However, the honey is still mainly what's being fermented.

MELOMELS. Meads made with other kinds of fruit than apples or grapes, such as raspberries, peaches and blackberries.

METHEGLIN. Spices—such as cloves, cinnamon, nutmeg or rosemary, to name a few—are often added to mead to create metheglin. Many popular meads incorporate spices, and metheglins are often enjoyed mulled in frosty weather.

Those interested in colonial-period British recipes for traditional mead and its kin would do well to look at *Wellcome Mead: 105 Mead Recipes from 17th and 18th Century English Receipt Manuscripts at the Wellcome Library*, edited by Laura D. Angotti. It includes much detail on the herbs that might be added, often for purported medicinal purposes, and some rarer ones, such as rue and winter savory.

Mead, though so long a popular beverage, found itself being replaced by cheap rum, much as honey was replaced by molasses. But it still had its fans. If one were to visit the port town of Alexandria in the spring in the early 1800s, it would be possible to visit a mead house:

MEAD, LEMONADE & CORDIALS.

The subscriber's Mead House is again open for the season, and he intends giving twelve tickets for one dollar, the bearer of which will be entitled to one bottle for each ticket—single bottle, the old established price of twelve and half cents—ice will be provided for those who may call for it, at his old establishment in Royal street, two doors above the Herald office, where he has for sale all kinds of Confectionary, and a quantity of Honey, by the bottle.
JOSEPH BOISEAU.
—Alexandria Gazette, *April 18, 1817*

One purveyor of mead went on to be prominent in a completely unrelated field. Dr. James Barclay opened an early drugstore in Charlottesville, and it had a mead fountain, along with a lot of other things:

DR. JAMES T. BARCLAY
offers for sale at his MEDICAL STORE, Charlottesville, VA., An extensive and choice assortment of MEDICINES, DRUGS, CHEMICALS, SURGICAL INSTRUMENTS, DYE-STUFFS, PAINTS, OILS, GLASS &C.
(WHOLESALE AND RETAIL.)
On very reduced terms. He is now receiving an additional supply from the Northern Markets, and will continue to receive and keep his assortment complete from the same source. physicians, apothecaries, merchants, and the public generally are respectfully invited to call and examine his stock, as he is confident they will find it in their interest to deal with him.

His SODA and MEAD FOUNTAINS will be kept in constant operation throughout the season; and he will continue to keep on hand a general supply of FRUITS, CONFECTIONARY, &C. and a variety of Fancy Articles.
—Virginia Advocate, *June 4, 1830*

Dr. Barclay was born in Hanover County. After his father died, his mother married a man who lived in Albemarle County. Shortly after opening the "medical store," Barclay married. The couple at first lived in downtown Charlottesville, but apparently the business thrived. Looking for a grander house, there was one on offer: Monticello, the home of the late president Thomas Jefferson. A devoted stepfather, he sent James to the relatively new University of Virginia. He lived there for a few years, entertaining visitors on occasion, one of whom was the noted clergyman Alexander Campbell, who was the founder of the Disciples of Christ Church, which abstains from alcohol.

Although having been raised a Presbyterian, Dr. Barclay converted to the new faith. He sold Monticello, and he and his family moved to Washington, where he turned his new home into a church. In 1850, he fulfilled a longtime wish and moved with his family to Jerusalem, where he gathered information for a book, returning to Jerusalem after it was published. He eventually returned to the United States to accept a teaching position at Bethany College, a school founded by Alexander Campbell.

Shepherdstown, located just across the Potomac River—and at that time still part of Virginia—was the location for a jolly confectionery, which also stocked mead and ale:

EAT, DRINK AND BE MERRY!
I would respectfully inform the citizens of Shepherdstown and vicinity that I have commenced the CONFECTIONARY BUSINESS and purpose keeping all that is necessary to please and gratify the taste. I will always have on hand Ale, Mead, Ice Creams, Frozen Ices, Candies, Cakes, Light Bread, Rolls, &c.
I have engaged the services of an experienced Baker and am prepared to supply private and public parties with everything they may wish.
Feeling sure of being able to gratify the most fastidious taste, I invite the Public to call, eat and grow fat. Room opposite Mr. Lambright's Hotel.
MRS. GREIST
—Shepherdstown Register, *May 8, 1858*

During Britain's Romantic period, there was a rise in interest in all things archaic, real or imagined, some of which found their way to the shores of America and into the columns of its newspapers:

> *Before the introduction of agriculture into Britain, says Dr. Henry, mead, that is honey diluted with water, and fermented, was probably the only strong liquor known to its inhabitants, as it was to many other nations in the same circumstances. This continued to be a favorite beverage amongst the ancient Britons, and their posterity, long after they had become acquainted with other liquors. The mead-maker was the eleventh person in dignity in the courts of the ancient princes of Wales, and took place of the physician.*
>
> *The following ancient law of that principality shows how much this liquor was esteemed by the princes: "There are three things in the Court which must be communicated to the King before they are made known to any other person; first, every sentence of the judge; second, every new song; and third, every cask of mead." This was, perhaps, the liquor which is called by Ossian the joy and strength of the shells* [sic], *with which his heroes were so much delighted. (History of Intoxicating Liquors.)*
> —Richmond Enquirer, *January 12, 1841*

Ancient royal connections aside, clearly mead (probably more properly metheglin) was still being made at home—and in quantity—as evidenced by this recipe printed in the *Shepherdstown Register* on June 19, 1885, for the delectation of housewives. The spice mace is the lacy outer portion of nutmeg and has a distinct taste.

> *MEAD. To twelve gallons of water, the whites of six eggs, well beaten, add twenty pounds of honey. let this boil an hour, then add cinnamon, ginger, cloves, mace and a little rosemary. When cold put a spoonful of yeast to it and stir it up; keep the vessel full as it works. When done working stop to close.*
> *Those who wished to bottle their own mead had convenient sources for supplies, should they make a trip to the capital:*
> *RICHMOND POTTERIES, Foot of Main Street, Rocketts, and Corner of Cary and 12 Streets, RICHMOND, VA. KEKSEE & PARR, Proprietors…they are manufacturing the best quality of STONE WARE, which they will sell at the following prices, with a liberal discount for cash…*
> *Beer or Mead Bottles, $9 per gross…*
> —Lynchburg Daily Virginian, *February 5, 1859*

By Any Other Name?

Meacham also referenced a kind of fermented beverage that was crushed or whole corn with some honey added. "Corn toddy" was popular in the early Chesapeake region but difficult to find in a modern equivalent.

Then there was "mead" made without a drop of honey:

A PALATABLE DRINK. Mr. Ezaras Z. Little hands us the following receipt for making a very superior Mead. Being frequently called on for a copy of the receipt, and he is disposed to give all the benefit of it:--Take five gallons milk warm water, five pounds white sugar, one quart hop sotz [rye bread], *one pint of hop water, three quarter ounce cream tartar, one ounce ginger and oil of lemon to suit the taste. Mix all together, and let them stand in the sun or in a warm place ten hours, then bottle and cork tightly.*
—Daily Express, *July 24, 1855*

As recorded in "Folk Medicine of the Pennsylvania Germans," non-English-speaking farmers, who had their own strong beekeeping traditions, also had their own honey beverages. Medittlum (metheglin) was made out of water and honeycombs from which the honey had been extracted. Garchel was a cordial was made out of honeycombs, water and brandy.

There was another sort of "mead" offered for sale that was hardly traditional in nature:

SUMMER DRINKS—Silver Medal premium MINERAL WATERS, Carbonated Champagne, and pure Crab CIDER, ALE AND PORTER, several varieties, all of them superior to and cheaper than any now to be had in town, TEMPERANCE CREAM MEAD, an excellent article for children and adults liable to constipation.
    LAGER BEER, now so highly recommended by Physicians. All the above articles for sale at our depot, No. 38, North Water street, Alexandria. EXCURSIONS and persons out of town, furnished on short notice, by leaving orders at the above place, with our wagon, or by mail.
ARNY & SHINN.
—Alexandria Gazette, *June 30, 1858*

"Temperance Cream Mead" would have been made without the kick of alcohol. The temperance movement, begun in the 1830s and finally carrying the day with Prohibition, eschewed any sort of intoxicating spirit, hence the beverage's recommendation as an excellent article for children.

THE DELIGHTS OF PEACH AND HONEY

Although not mead, one honey-based beverage was so popular in Virginia that deserves special mention. Virginia's dark-minded poetic son, Edgar Allan Poe, was supposed to have tippled it during his abbreviated stay at the University of Virginia.

How was it made? Here's one way:

> [To turn]…*peaches into brandy…the fruit* [is] *allowed to get dead-ripe on the trees, then mashed to a pulp in the cider trough, and put into stands to ferment, then duly distilled. Barreled, after two years in the lumber house, it was racked into clean barrels, and some part of it converted into "peach and honey," the favorite gentleman's tipple. Strained honey was mixed with brandy in varying proportions—the amount depending somewhat upon individual tastes. Some used one measure of honey to three of brandy, others put one to two, still others half and half, qualifying the sweetness by adding neat brandy at the time of drinking. Peach and honey was kept properly in stone jugs or in demijohns, improved mightily with age, and was, at its best, to the last degree insidious. Newly mixed it was heady, but after a year or more, as smooth as oil, and as mellow. The honey had something to do with final excellence. That which the bees gathered from wild raspberries in flower, being very clear, light-colored and fine-flavored, was in especial request.*
> —Dishes & Beverages of the Old South, *243–44*

Distilleries were common on plantations. *History and Old Homes of King William County* mentions Butler Edwards, born at Forest Villa in 1800. He married but had no children and devoted his time "principally to fox hunting and outdoor pleasures." He did have a large distilling plant, and his peach and honey was a "celebrated beverage."

Peach and honey did have staying power. An advertisement in the December 26, 1909 issue of the *Daily Press* included it in a sales listing for "THE BEST WINES AND LIQUORS FOR THE LEAST MONEY":

SPECIAL HOLIDAY PRICES OFFERED IN PERSON
Jamaica Rum, gal …. $2.50
New England Rum, Gal …. $2.00
Peach and Honey, gal …. $1.00

Mead Makes a Comeback

After many years of obscurity, true mead has reclaimed its place as a spirited craft beverage. As Roger A. Morse writes in his *Making Mead (Honey Wine): History, Recipes, Methods and Equipment*, one early incentive for the modern meadery was finding a use for the honey crop after the wars were over and with them the sugar shortages, so the price of honey dropped considerably.

Today, there are numerous meaderies throughout Virginia.

One of the oldest of this new vintage is Misty Mountain Meadworks, just outside of Winchester, Virginia. Owner Richard Copeland was turned on to mead while taking classes in medieval studies at college. His professor shared some of his historically inspired homebrew. Copeland experimented with methods and ingredients for decades. The resulting mead and metheglin (mead made with spice) and melomel (mead made with fruit) are sweet without being cloying and reminded this author of what might have been served by Tolkien's elves. Misty Mountain's products are available by mail order and in certain shops or can be picked up at the meadery by prior arrangement.

While in Williamsburg, the mead-minded may care to stop at Silver Hand Meadery. Owner Glenn Lavender was inspired by the historical novels of Stephen Lawhead—read while spending twelve years on the road with his band—to re-create the mead he had read about. Silver Hand's product won six gold medals at the 2021 Virginia Governor's Cup competition. Silver Hand's creations are available at its store and other brick-and-mortar outlets as well as online at silverhandmeadery.com.

Black Heath Meadery in Richmond offers meads both traditional and modern—and some are carbonated. Owner Bill Cavender participates in numerous community events and created a mead based on a recipe from *The Frugal Housewife: Or, Complete Woman Cook* (1802) for a special tasting in conjunction with the Virginia Historical Society, now the Virginia Museum of History and Culture.

Virginia's Mead Path

There is a wine trail in Virginia, but there also seems to be a mead path. Here is a list of active meaderies in Virginia, as of this writing, with apologies to anyone missed. Some are open only seasonally, so please do check websites for current information.

The Display Room at Silver Hand Meadery, Williamsburg, Virginia. *Photo by Autumn Chen.*

Aethling Meadworks | Roanoke | www.aethlingmead.com
Black Heath Meadery | Richmond | www.blackheathmeadery.com
Blacksnake Meadery | Dugspur (Carroll County) | www.blacksnakemead.com
Capital Hive Meadery | Leesburg | www.capitalmeadery.com
Funktastic Meads | Amherst | www.facebook.com/funktasticmeads
Haley's Honey Meadery and Gift Shop | Hopewell | www.
   haleyshoneymeadery.com
Hill Top Berry Farm & Winery | Nellysford (Nelson County) | www.
   hilltopberrywine.com
Hinson Ford Cider and Mead | Amissville (Rappahannock County) |
   www.hinsonford.com

Beekeeping for Silver Hand Meadery & Honey Shop. *Courtesy of Consociate Media.*

Left: Silver Hand Meadery & Honey Shop, Williamsburg, Virginia. *Photo by Autumn Chen.*

Right: Educational Materials at Silver Hand Meadery, Williamsburg, Virginia. *Photo by Autumn Chen.*

Honey & Hops Brew Works | Front Royal |
   www.honeyandhopsbrewworks.com
Honey Grail | Leesburg | www.honeygrail.com
Misty Mountain Meadworks | Winchester | www.mistymountainmead.com
Saga Meadery & Winery | Front Royal | www.sagameadery.com
Serendipity Meadworks | Smithfield | www.serendipitymeadworks.com
Silver Hand Meadery | Williamsburg | www.silverhandmeadery.com
Stonehouse Meadery | Purcellville (Loudoun County) |
   stonehousemeadery.com
The Thistle & Stag Meadery | Fork Union | www.thistleandstag.com
Windchaser Meadery | Williamsburg | www.windchasermeadery.com

SCIENTIFIC AMERICANS
AND THEIR BEES

The Congress shall have Power...To promote the Progress of Science and useful Arts, by securing for limited Times to Authors and Inventors the exclusive Right to their respective Writings and Discoveries.
—The Constitution of the United States, Article 1, Section 8

The United States Patent Office began its work in 1790. Patents have been around since medieval times, and even as a young country—the patent office began before there was national patent law—America had a clear need to at least attempt to allow inventors to reap some reward for their efforts.

"Blake's Patent Beehive" made the registry list in 1820, put forth by Edward Blake of Hartford County, Maine. There may have been earlier hives registered, but the 1836 U.S. Patent Office fire destroyed thousands of documents (even though a fire station was close by, there were no firemen available to assist), so researchers do not know for certain. Patents issued before the fire caused laudatory changes in record keeping, making post-conflagration discoveries easier to reference. Understandably, today's online records add a significant layer of accessibility. The curious can search for what patent records there are via patents.google.com.

The paper fire went out, but the intellectual fire did not. By the end of the 1830s, several beehive patents had made their way through the U.S. Patent Office and then onto the Virginia market, such as this one from Samuel Morrill of Maine:

store are increased." When the centre box is filled, access to the super and one side-box may be given by opening the slides. The glass is likely to be filled first, if kept warm by suitable coverings, and can be removed when the honey is sealed in the combs. If the season be very productive, one or both of the side-boxes may also be taken before the end of the summer, if sufficient stores are left in the

FIG. 47.—MODERN HIVES. NUTT'S COLLATERAL HIVE IN THE FOREGROUND.

central stock-portion, or if any deficiency be made up by judicious feeding.

The next and most important modification to which we come is the introduction of movable frames into hives, admitting of separate removal, either for examination as to conditions, or for the taking of honey. Bevan—whose admirable work on *The Honey Bee,* published nearly half a century ago, is the foundation of modern systems of apiculture in this country—

"Modern Hives. Nutt's collateral Hive is in the Foreground." From *The Honey-bee; Its Nature, Homes and Products*, by W.H. Harris, 1884. *Biodiversity Heritage Library.*

Staunton Spectator & General Advertiser, *Volume 16, Number 10, 31 January 1839. pg. 4*

HONEY! HONEY!
Patent Bee Hive.
WILLIAM D. COOKE

Would respectfully inform those who are interested in the growing of Bees, or who are fond of good HONEY, that he has the right for making, using, and vending to others to be used, in the county of Augusta, Morrill's PATENT BEE HIVE—This Hive is so constructed that the Bees work in glass vessels, or common glass tumblers—is a complete preventive to the Web Worm, Moth, and other destructive insects; the vessels can be taken away at any time without interrupting the Bees, thus rendering unnecessary the most cruel practice of destroying these useful insects. The Honey made in these Hives is of a far superior quality to that made in the common hives, as there is a place prepared in the interior of the Patent Hive where the Bees deposit their young, bread, and winter store. All those who have heretofore debarred the pleasure and benefit of raising their own Honey, on account of the difficulties of protecting their Bees from the ravages of the Web-worm and Moth, may be assured that this Hive affords perfect protection to the Bee against all its enemies.

TESTIMONIALS.

Nelson Co., Va. Sept. 25th 1838
I have seen Morrill's Patent Bee Hive in full operation in the city of Washington, examined two Glass Jars wherein the Honey comb was deposited, and am of opinion, that for simplicity of construction, utility and economy, it exceeds anything of the kind I have ever seen.
H. Garland.

Warrenton, Fauquier Co., Va.
June 12, 1837
Mr. Bayliss—Sir—I take pleasure in informing you, and those who are interested in the rearing of Bees, that I have one of your patent Hives in full operation in my garden. I am fully satisfied of its utility, and with confidence

recommend it to my friends and the public; as I am now convinced it will answer a most desirable purpose. I wish you success,
JOHN R. TONGUE.

We concur with John R. Tongue in the opinions expressed.
A.J. Marshall
John H. Digges
Wm. T. Randolph,
Wm. S. Kemper

"Beemen" and the Discovery of Bee Space

One of the most significant developments for agriculture, apiary agriculture in particular, although all growers would benefit, was the discovery of "bee space." Until the nineteenth century, what had been missed was knowledge of the optimum space between combs. Too much, and the bees would try to make more comb between the bars to make the most use of space, resulting in combs that were difficult if not impossible for beekeepers to remove. If there were too little space, the bees could not work it properly and instead would seal the space with propolis, again making them difficult to maneuver. Given the correct spacing, bees would work the comb fruitfully without building on additions or making repairs that were not up to the beekeepers' optimum code.

As is the case with major advancements, discoveries lead to improved discoveries. Although Reverend Langstroth is best known in America for bee space, which allowed for moveable hives, François Huber of Switzerland had already devised a hive in 1789 whose frames opened like the pages of a book. Reverend Langstroth acknowledged that without Huber's invention, he would not have thought that frames could be removed without enraging the bees.

According to the *American Bee Journal*'s site, in 1851, its future first editor, Samuel Wagner, was convinced to visit Reverend Langstroth by a fellow clergyman who had seen Langstroth's newly invented hive. Wagner had already agreed to translate into English and publish Silesian (now part of Poland) Johann Dzierzon's *Rational Beekeeping*, but, having seen the fellow American's system at work, it was Langstroth's hive that he ultimately promoted. He found it to be superior, although he did translate Dzierzon's book into English as promised. Dzierzon, as well as other innovative European beekeepers, had already made use of bee space in their hives, but it had not found its way to America. A difference between Langstroth's hives and the European was that his opened from the top, whereas theirs were accessed from the side, a better choice, as they were more likely to be kept in bee houses than in the relative open. Langstroth's reckoning for the top bee space accordingly allowed for easy release from the Langstroth hive, as it was called. He had great respect for Dzierzon, who is generally acknowledged as the father of modern apiculture, not only for his hive designs but also for his biological discoveries, including drones' emergence from unfertilized eggs.

Wagner convinced Reverend Langstroth to write his own book. With the help of his wife, Anne Tucker Langstroth, the clergyman penned *Langstroth on the Hive and the Honeybee, A Bee-Keeper's Manual*, which was published in 1853 to an enthusiastic reception. It is still in print today, although out-of-copyright editions may be found online.

Reverend Langstroth predicted that America would have its own bee journal, just as Germany had, to serve as "a most powerful influence in disseminating information, awakening enthusiasm, and guarding the public against the miserable impositions to which it has so long been subjected."

As noted in *Sweet Stuff: An American History of Sweeteners*, Americans made close to 15 million pounds of honey in 1850 and over 23 million pounds in 1860. As the honey harvest grew through innovations, so did the public's interest in apiculture.

Less than ten years later, on the eve of the Civil War, the *American Bee Journal* published its first issue. It lasted for a year before wartime realities put it on hiatus until July 1866. It continues to flourish to the present, a mirror for its times and a spotlight for innovations as well as a font of wisdom. Langstroth remained in close association with the journal until his death in 1895. Johann Dzierzon also contributed articles, as did many other well-known "beemen," including French expatriate Charles Dadant.

Frank Chapman Pellett, who would later serve as its field editor and associate editor and who also authored *The History of American Beekeeping*, remarked:

> *The history of the* American Bee Journal *has been the history of the rise of beekeeping, and the one is inseparably linked to that of the other. Before*

this first copy of the first bee magazine in the English language appeared, there were few of the implements now in common use among beekeepers. Conventions of beemen had not been held, a practical smoker had not yet been invented, queen excluders were unknown, comb foundation was still to be perfected, the extractor had not come into use, nor had commercial queen rearing been suggested.

Success breeds competition, and so it was with American beekeeping publications. *Gleanings in Bee Culture*, first published by A.I. Root & Company in Medina, Ohio, in 1874 enlightened readers on new developments and offered a convenient portal to purchase everything from frames to colonies to new-fangled smokers to beekeeping clothing. Like *American Bee Journal*, it kept step with the times. The early 1990s saw a name change to *Bee Culture: The Magazine of American Beekeeping*. Other early American titles included *The Bee-Keeper's Magazine* (1872–1882) and *The Bee-Keepers' Review* (1888–1916). Naturally, there were titles that were more academic in nature, and there was no shortage of overseas publications. Honey was flowing more richly than ever.

Formal smokers were a topic of great interest, as it had long been known that smoke calmed the bees, making them far easier to work with. According to *The World History of Beekeeping and Honey Hunting*, bellows-style smokers had been in use in Europe since 1771, but their emission was rather small and was not known in the United States. As late as the 1865 edition, Langstroth's book recommended blowing smoke gently on the bees from a piece of rotten wood.

New York beekeeper Moses Quinby, a contributor to the *American Bee Journal* and considered by many to be the father of commercial and practical beekeeping in America, devised a one-handed bellows smoker in 1873—a design he improved upon over time. Quinby, who had a high regard for the

Advertisement for A.I. Root's Bee Supplies Catalog. *From the* American Bee Journal *(January 1891).*

From The ABC of Bee Culture... *by A.I. Root, 1884.*

profitability beekeepers might enjoy, had already established his reputation with his handbook *Mysteries of Bee-Keeping Explained* (1853).

The method of extracting honey from the comb was something else that needed improvement if honey harvests were to increase. An Austrian officer born in Bohemia, Franz Hruschka (1819–1888), devised the first form of the centrifugal extractor while living in Venice. He presented the invention at the 1865 Brno (now in the Czech Republic) Beekeeper Conference. The traditional story is that he offered his son a piece of comb honey, and the boy, being playful, spun it around in circles. His father noticed that the spinning force released the honey from the comb. However, author Eva Crane noted that Major Hruschka was living near a molasses factory at the time, so it is possible he observed a similar method being used to separate liquid molasses from its crystallized portion and that was the inspiration.

In any event, the honey extractor and its improvements from later inventive beekeepers allowed them to save the bees' energy from having to make fresh comb every season. This made beekeeping potentially even more profitable. There was a small problem, however. Customers were used to buying their

"Moses Quinby" in *The New Bee-keepers' Text-book. Biodiversity Heritage Library.*

honey in the comb and questioned whether honey without the comb was truly honey at all. They had reason to be skeptical, as some honey sharks had found ways to counterfeit the good stuff, sometimes dropping a piece of comb in a jar to trick the eye and add a little more flavor. Then, there was the problem of crystallization. Customers complained that there was something wrong with the separated honey as it crystallized over time, when that is just a natural process that can be undone by warming the jar gently in a water bath.

Because beeswax is also a valuable commodity, it was not always desirable to reuse honeycomb. Comb foundation, another European invention, gave bees a welcome starting point to produce fresh comb, and this also saved time and money. Americans added a few twists, such as shallow, hexagonal cell walls, and used a roller device to press the design into a sheet of wax.

An Opinion to the Contrary

T.B. (Thomas B.) Miner (1808–1878) published his book, *The American Bee Keeper's Manual…*, before the Langstroth book came into print. He was also the publisher of *The Rural American*, published 1856–1869. This self-assured editorial from that serial was reprinted in the *Shenandoah Herald* on July 2, 1879, for the edification of Valley beekeepers:

"Fallacies in Bee-Keeping" by T.B. Miner

One would suppose that the beekeepers of the United States had had sufficient experience to settle down on established rules for the management of bees; but instead of this, we continually find in the correspondence of the bee magazines contradictory theories and statements, to such an extent that a beginner in the business would be led to suppose that the management of the bees was in its infancy and that scarcely anything pertaining thereto had become established beyond all doubt. The following are a few examples of the fallacies that are extent in regard to apiculture.

bees will fall into the hive. Comparatively few will fly, the vastly larger proportion having clung too tightly to one another readily to disengage themselves. As soon as possible, a floor-board should be quietly and gently placed over the open end of the skep, which must now be inverted, so as to rest on the board. One side may be slightly propped, to

FIG. 62.—HIVING A SWARM.

afford the flying bees opportunity of more speedy admission to the interior than the ordinary entrance hole would give them. Another quarter of an hour or twenty minutes will suffice for all but a small number of stragglers to join their companions inside. Meantime, a shade should be again provided, till all have entered.

N 2

"Hiving a swarm." From *The Honey-bee; Its Nature, Homes and Products*, by W.H. Harris. *Biodiversity Heritage Library.*

"The Italian bees are now universally admitted to be far superior to our native blacks." This is not true, as the testimony of bee-keepers generally is about equally divided on the subject; and some skilled bee keepers claim our native bees to be the best.

"The Langstroth frame has come almost into universal use." The facts are, that not one-tenth of the bee keepers of this country use them, because they find other shapes and sizes more profitable.

"It is expected that all apiarists will clip all queens' wings as soon as they get to laying, thereby saving all loss of swarms by flight to the woods." Bad advice; better not "tinker" too much with bees. How many swarms go to the woods when the queens' wings are not cut? Not one in twenty-five, if one provides good clustering bushes, the best being cedar, or hemlock branches tied to stakes around the apiary. Then, no natural swarms can be obtained with the queens crippled.

"All queens should be changed in the month of June to prevent increase in swarms." All bosh. Mr. Doolittle cites a case in which a "noted bee keeper made this experiment at the cost of nearly his whole honey crop." It is but little labor to keep bees. If one lets them take care of themselves, it does not require much labor to attend to them; but as a business to support a family, a man will find that he has got to work, and keep his eyes wide open, as regards the condition of his bees.

"I killed twenty-seven fertile workers in a nucleus of 1,000 bees." So says a bee-keeper. A fertile worker bee is one that is supposed to have been fed on a portion of the "royal jelly" that makes queens. Whether they are thus fed in the embryo state by accident, mistake, or otherwise, is not known yet our most scientific bee keepers, after a life spent in apiarian researches, have failed to see a fertile worker, but the above party "killed twenty-seven" in a little "nucleus of 1,000 bees!" Mr. Moses Quinby, a short time before his death, in a published article said in regard to this class of bees, "I never saw one," the great difficulty being in discovering them, that they are exactly like the common workers. Now, the idea that a man could single out twenty-seven fertile workers in a few minutes and kill them, is the grossest kind of humbuggery.

"The honey must be extract(ed) from the central combs in the fall, or the bees will not winter well." This fallacy is also being published "in the papers," is being claimed that empty combs are warmer than those filled with honey and capped over, but taking away the honey from the immediate vicinity of the cluster is the worst thing that can be done, because in very cold weather the bees must have honey where they are clustered, or they will perish if the weather continues cold several weeks.

"As early in the season as we are able to obtain queens, we must requeen all ours stocks." The sapient bee-keeper who wrote this said it must be done because "no queen will be as fertile the second as the first year." How has he proved this? It never has been so proved by any evidence worth a straw. I deny the assertion, and call for the proof that I am wrong. Probably the man who claims that all stocks must be re-queened raises queens to sell.

"Fifteen years ago, someone made the discovery that the fertilization of the queen could be confined to three or four selected drones!" Nobody ever made any such "discovery" and never will, as the nature of the honey bee, as regards the fertilization of queens by drones on the wing, high in the air, will forever be a bar to any such thing. I do not say that the writer of the above intended to deceive people, but merely that he is mistaken.

"We can work our bees to good advantage by putting their extracted honey into combs." That is, at a certain season of the year, take the honey that has previously been extracted (a few weeks before) and feed to the bees to make comb honey! What next? The bee-keepers of this country after extracting the honey stored in the brood combs, will probably think that feeding it back to the bees is not advisable; and that such an operation will not pay.

"Queens after the third year lay drone eggs only." I deny the truth of this assertion, and call for the proof that it is true, if anybody can adduce it. If it were true, a great many families of bees would consist wholly of drones; and in forty years of bee-keeping I never saw such a family.

"I think it would be a good plan to pedigree our queens." So said a man who is probably non compos mentis, and his friends had better look after him.

There are many men, who have kept bees two or three years, who think they know all there is to be learned about them. Another class, who have kept them eight or ten years, begin to see that they don't know as much as they thought they did; and another class, who have studied the nature and habits of bees twenty years, freely admit that there are many things pertaining to them that no man can fathom—The Rural New Yorker

THE PATENT OFFICE WAS ABUZZ

While all this innovation and increased production was going on, Virginians—whether come-heres or natives—were busy at the patent office, too.

James E. Ross: Storekeeper and Postmaster

James Ervin Ross (1813–1861) served as postmaster in Mount Sidney, Augusta County, as recorded in the 1853, 1856 and 1857 editions of the U.S. Postal Directory. More than ten years earlier, he had put in an application for a patent on a beehive improvement to the hive's stand, which also added a tinplate for making allowing or hindering bees' movement as desired. According to the 1860 census, he was a merchant, with real estate valued at $2,000 and a personal estate valued at $10,000. He died before shots were fired at the First Battle of Manassas and is buried in Bells Cemetery in Mount Sidney.

His modest home, much modernized, still stands at 2359A Lee Highway in the Mount Sidney Historic District, as does his store at 2353 Lee Highway. The Virginia Landmarks Register files tell the neighborhood's history and purpose:

Mount Sidney Historic District was established in 1826, making it one of the oldest towns in the county. It originally consisted of a few residences and commercial establishments, most of which served the needs of travelers along the Old Wagon Road. The town experienced a building boom in the 1830s when the Old Wagon Road was improved as the Valley Turnpike. After the Civil War, the Valley Railroad arrived just east of town, bringing residents more access to wider markets and cementing the town's reputation as one of the leading commercial centers in northern Augusta County. Today the community is an excellent example of a well-preserved turnpike town in the Shenandoah Valley, containing examples of vernacular architecture from the early 19th century to the mid-20th century.

Generous George Calvert and His "Bee Palace"

In Fauquier County, there lived a man who was known for his honey and his beehives. George Calvert (1795–1871) and his hives (patented 1853) were frequently written of:

HONEY—Mr. George Calvert, of Upperville, Va., who received a silver medal from his bee palace, and premiums for his honey taken from different hives at the recent exhibition of the Mechanics' Institute of this City, is a Virginian, every inch of him, though endowed with all that "go ahead activeness" in matters of mechanical improvements, so peculiarly the characteristics of the New Englander. His bee palace is now admitted to be the best contrivance for securing the largest yield of honey, as well as the clearest and cleanest yield, that has ever been invented. All who have tried it (and a great many improving agriculturalists in all quarters of the Union, have already availed themselves of it,) unite to certify its immeasurable superiority over any and all other contrivances to the same end heretofore known. It can be used in the heart of any city. The present Mayor of Boston, famous for his thorough knowledge of the habits of the bee, and for his success in raising large quantities of honey in the heart of the great city in which he resides, has triumphantly demonstrated that fact. With

one of Mr. Calvert's bee palaces, any family in Washington may secure for themselves from 150 to 250 pounds of honey per annum, without a dollar of additional cost, and with the but the application and care of the female members of the family circle. It can be seen on exhibition at the Patent Office for a few days only.
—Evening Star *(Washington, D.C.) March 17, 1855*

His improved hive was constructed so that "the litter is all freely and certainly passed off, and said bottom is as nearly as possible conformed to the position in which the bees naturally work their comb, breed their young, and congregate themselves together in winter, so that there is rendered thereby less unoccupied space for the cold air in winter, thereby securing more certainly the health of the colony through the winter." Calvert's design also had an eye to managing swarms and preventing wax moth worm.

As noted elsewhere, on the eve of war, the honey business was in fine fettle, with large quantities of Virginia honey being shipped out of state. Nonetheless, Calvert did not neglect his friends at the newspaper:

HONEY.—Mr. George Calvert, of Upperville, Fauquier County, yesterday presented us with a box of most beautiful and delicious honey, a sample of about one and a half tons, that he brought down, and a greater portion of which will be taken to New York. This honey was made in Mr. C.'s patent hives, which have taken the premium from Virginia to Vermont, and are conceded to be the best now in use. For the information of those of our citizens who wish to procure some of this honey we will state that it can be had at the Agricultural warhouse [sic] of Mr. W.H. May, where Mr. Calvert has left some for sale, neatly put up in tin boxes of convenient sizes.
—Alexandria Gazette, *November 20, 1860*

Toward the end of his life, having survived the war (as well as a train wreck in 1853), Calvert made an effort to see that his patented hives had wider use. Once more, the *Alexandria Gazette* was there to set it in the record:

HONEY.—Mr. George Calvert, of Upperville, Va., is now at the City Hall with specimens of his patent bee hives and samples of the honey made in them. He has just returned from a trip of over two thousand miles, during which he has disposed of many State, country and

individual rights to his valuable improvement. The hives are certainly the most conveniently arranged of any others ever seen in this section of the country, and the large quantity of honey in them is clear and beautiful. Mr. Calvert will remain here several days.
—Alexandria Gazette, *June 6, 1870*

Asa Blood Traveled Far

Asa Blood Sr., surely a name to conjure with, patented his beehive in 1858, when he was living in Norfolk, Virginia. The nature of his invention was the construction of a hive where "the breeding bees are separated from the working bees while the honey made can be removed without disturbing the bees." It also allowed old comb to be cleaned out readily. Like many with inventive minds, Blood did not stop with one device. He obtained additional patents for a steam heating stove, a washing machine and a dredging machine.

Blood's life was full of trying new things. According to Roger Deane Harris's *The Story of the Bloods…*, Asa Blood Sr. was born about 1800 in New York State. He traveled to Wisconsin in 1836, and he and his family were the first residents there of European descent. He left the house he built on the north bank of Honey Creek. Having sold a mill site there as part of a partnership, he is next recorded in Sugar Creek in June 1837, living in a log house. Apparently, conditions were rather spartan, as it was noted, "My informant says he dined there on a certain occasion, his bill of fare running thus: 'Boiled Beans; and beans only, minus salt.'"

In June 1848, he and his son, Asa Jr., were prospecting for a home in Independence, Iowa, but he was discouraged by malarial fever. In 1851, he set out for Norfolk, Virginia, without his son, who had stayed in Independence to work as a mason, as well as a hunter and trapper, before moving on to become wealthy in mining operations and eventually patenting a few inventions himself.

John K. Leedy: Bees in the Parlor and a Vision

About the same time Asa Blood was getting a patent for his beehive, John K. Leedy of Tom's Brook, Woodstock, Virginia, in Shenandoah County, sent in an application for his version, which he received on July 12, 1859. He was as interested in form as in function:

My invention is designed to inaugurate a new method in the art of preserving bees and expedite the process of taking the honey. The hive may be so constructed as to represent a handsome piece of furniture, which can then be placed in your own room or parlor without the slightest possibility of the bees ever disturbing you. The honey can be removed without fear and you can at all times have the operations of the bees immediately under your own observation and superintendence.

John Waller Palmer (1827–1919) of Port Republic in Rockingham County worked in tandem with Leedy on a beehive design in 1860. Today, Aylett Apiaries, owned by another John W. Palmer, is producing local honey in King William County, Virginia.

Tom's Brook, Leedy's hometown, became the site of the largest cavalry battle in the Shenandoah Valley on October 9, 1864, according to the Shenandoah at War website. The battle was also known as Woodstock Races for the Union's successful rout of the overextended Confederate cavalry.

In later years, Leedy, a Dunkard preacher, was living in Roanoke, Virginia, in a second-story apartment. He was still applying for patents, including one for a railway light in 1902. It was his proposition for another invention that caught the local newsman's jaundiced eye:

Shenandoah Herald, *Woodstock, Virginia, 9/4/1903*
UNSINKABLE SHIP SEEN IN DREAM

Roanoke, Va., Aug. 16.—John K. Leedy, a Dunkard preacher 75 years of age, a native of Rockingham county, this state, and for many years a well-known citizen and familiar figure on the streets of this city, is, without doubt, one of the greatest believers in dreams that ever lived. Through what he claims to be a divine inspiration he has been enabled to invent the "Leedy unsinkable ship." This man of the Word does not propose to keep his gold mine bottled up, but in order that his fellow countrymen may reap a harvest of sheckles [sic] and be rich beyond the dream of avarice he has seen fit to organize the "Compressed Air Ship Company," with a capital stock of $1,500,000. A charter has already been granted by the state of South Dakota, the paper bearing the signature of O.S. Berg, secretary of that commonwealth.

Mr. Leedy is not the only Virginian who has unbounded faith in dreams, for since relating to his friends and acquaintances his remarkable *vision they have come forward and deposited something over $31,000 in the coffers of the reverend prophet, for which they have received certificates of stock duly signed by the officers of the company.*

The Inventor at Home

Mr. Leedy lives in an apartment over a small fruit store on East Campbell avenue, just off Market square. When the reporter sought to find his place of abode and inquired of several boys at the street entrance to a flight of outside steps leading to the second floor if he was on the right trail of the compressed air ship man they replied: "There's an old gentleman what keeps a bank stays up there." Once gaining the rickety landing at the top, a rap on the door was answered by an invitation to "come in," Mr. Leedy was found seated by a window in his bed chamber, reading his bible. When he was told that the purpose of the call was to learn something of his ship a broad smile stole over the aged preacher-inventor's face, his eyes sparkled and the proffered hand of the visitor was given a hearty shake. The anticipation of the possible sale of a good-sized block of stock to the man with the interrogation points had, no doubt, engendered the happiness which was boldly written on the dreamer's countenance.

"I am glad you have come to see me," said the patentee of the remarkable craft, "for I can show you the greatest thing in the world and demonstrate with a small model its absolute worth."

Exhibits a Model

He crossed the room to a small table on which stands a compressed air drum, and attached to which is one end of a rubber tube, the other end being connected at the side of the two gallon can which is submerged in a twenty gallon tank of water. When the valve of the air drum was turned on the air was forced into the side of the can and displaced the water, which went out through a small hole in the bottom and can immediately made its appearance on the surface, where it remained until a stopper in the top was removed. The air escaped and the can again slowly filled with water from the hole in the bottom, and soon was out of sight.

The operation was repeated several times and afforded evident pleasure to the gray-haired dreamer scientist.

Asked how he had come to contrive the ship, Mr. Leedy replied:

"Several years ago, just after one of the big ocean liners loaded with human freight went to the bottom of the Atlantic ocean and all on board were lost, I had a dream. In this dream I talked to an angel, the messenger of God painted a large picture of a ship and commanded me to set about and construct such a vessel for the good of mankind. I thought but little of the dream until two three nights afterward when the angel again appeared and directed me to do as I had been told, and for a second time a large picture of a ship, which was to be my model, was painted. I gave the matter more serious thought on the following day, and for several nights thereafter my dreams were of nothing but the ship. I read my Bible and found certain passages which told me I must get to work. The result of my labors is what will be known to the world as 'Leedy's unsinkable ship.'

You ask me to describe this great lifesaving invention."

How Ship Is Built

"The hull is comprised of an outer and inner casing, the inner casing composed of copper plates, soldered together, thus making it water and air-tight. Between the outer and inner casing from a short distance above the lower deck there is place a filling of coal tar or some other suitable material. The lower deck is composed of two layers of metal soldered together thus making the hold of the vessel air-tight.

"Between the ribs of the vessel and between the outer and inner casings above the lower deck are the empty spaces which are adapted to be closed by air-tight coverings, and communicating with these spaces are tubes for supplying compressing air in the space, the air being supplied by an air compressing engine on the main deck.

"On both sides of the ship and outside of the hull are arranged a series of bags which can be run up and down the sides of the vessel by means of a chin [chain] and pulley on each side. Should the ship run on a sand bar or rock those bags may be sent to the bottom of the ship there filled with compressed air, thus lifting the ship off the bar or rock.

"The coal bunkers and various other compartments aboard the ship are adapted to be transformed into compressed air chambers at will, so it is seen that, even though the ship would spring a leak of a very serious nature, her bilge pumps and many air chambers would prevent her sinking. Her hold, on account of its air and water-tight construction, would be a vast air tank that would be impossible to sink.

Has Secured Patents

"What about my patents? Well I have already taken out patents in the United States, Great Britain and Canada, and expect to secure patents in every country on the globe. God fixed the capital of the company in this country at $1,500,000. When that amount has been raised, we will erect vast shipyards in some seaport town and begin the immediate construction of the vessels. Once our machinery is in motion, there will be a wild scramble of the millionaires to invest in our stock and buy the ships. John Pierpont Morgan will get on his knees and try to crowd up to the front, so eager will he and his like be to get possession of a boat that will not sink, no matter how many holes she has in her hull. The great warships of the world, along with every other craft that now sails the seas and rivers, will be broken up and sold for junk. No more lives will be lost at sea. I expect to live to see my invention put into use, and will then be content to pass to the one who has given me this wonderful power to save untold millions of lives that otherwise would find water graves. Some wiseacres turn up their noses and hoot at the feasibility of the thing, but doesn't worry me one bit. God has pointed out the way, and I know I am right."

When questioned as to what success he was having in disposing of stock, Mr. Leedy produced a certificate book and exhibited stubs which represented more than $31,000 already sold. This stock has been purchased chiefly by people living in Roanoke, Franklin and Botetourt counties, this state. The list of names includes men in all walks of life, among them being ministers, merchants and other substantial citizens, the majority of them being very religiously inclined.

"What will you do with the many millions which will be derived from this great invention?" was the next query put to the venerable dreamer, and to which he answered:

"Oh, well, that's hard to tell just now. I don't expect to get all the profits, you know. I am selling the stock to anybody who wishes it. Of course, though being at the head of the concern, naturally I will reserve a large lump of the holdings. There's always some place to put money to good use, and I shall derive great pleasure in giving my profits for the relief of suffering humanity. The only determined plan I have at present, however, is to erect a monument to myself on the very spot in Rockingham county where I first saw the crack of dawn."

The man who had sought light went out again into the mart; the man who had found it dropped back into his easy chair, took up his worn Bible and resumed reading.

The HMS *Titanic* was launched nine years later. At one point, John Pierpont Morgan—who owned the White Star Line's parent company—was on the passenger list, but business interests caused him to take a different voyage.

John H. Baker and Isaac P. Baldwin, Union Men

To all whom it may concern:
Be it known that we, JOHN H. BAKER and ISAAC P. BALDWIN, respectively of Broadway and Manassas, in the counties of Rockingham and Prince William and State of Virginia, have invented certain new and useful Improvements in Bee-Hives 5 and we do hereby declare the following to be a full, clear, and exact description of the invention, such as will enable others skilled in the art to which it pertains to make and use it, reference being had to the accompanying drawings, which form part of this specification.

Our invention relates to an improvement in bee-hives; and it consists in the arrangement and combination of parts, that will be more fully described hereinafter, whereby a cheap, simple, and effective hive is produced, that will allow a free access to its interior at all times, permit the bees to be watched, or to see whether moths or millers have gotten in, and enable the doors to be used as a means of hanging the honey-frames on while the lower part of the hive is being inspected.
(Specification forming part of Letters Patent No. 186098, dated January 9, 1877 application filed December 2, 1876.)

The two men who came together to create this patented beehive were both interested in education—and staunch Unionists—although one was born in the heart of Virginia. John H. Baker of Broadway in Rockingham County left his home for Iowa during the war. While there, he supplied the Union army with thousands of pounds of tobacco, for which he petitioned reimbursement after the war. He received an initial payment of $173.75.

Shortly after his patent venture, Baker became a salesman for a dictionary of practical knowledge:

> *John H. Baker, of Broadway, is agent for Rockingham county for the sale of Youman's Dictionary of Everyday Wants, and is actively engaged in canvassing for the work. He will visit Harrisonburg soon for the same purpose.*

Youman's Dictionary* is a valuable book. In it the professional man, the mechanic, the farmer, the housekeeper, the merchant, in fact, everybody, can find valuable information, and it will be a great addition to any library.

If anything is desired to be done, which is not exactly understood, a reference to this Dictionary will tell how to do it, and the latest and best improvement in methods. "How to know everything" would be an appropriate title for the book as it embraces almost every variety of subjects.

It contains 539 pages, and is sold at the low price of from $4 to $4.75, according to binding. It is sold only by agents, and, if the book is not as represented by them, subscribers are not obliged to take it.

—*The* Old Commonwealth *(Harrisonburg, VA), September 26, 1878*
*Readers can find a link to the online edition in the bibliography

Baker did not stay in Virginia. By the time the second bill for his relief, which amounted to more than $1,500, came through Congress in the early 1900s, Baker had moved out of state.

His co-inventor Isaac P. Baldwin left a few more traces of his life in his adopted hometown. Baldwin moved to Manassas shortly after the close of the Civil War. At one time, he was the largest individual real estate holder and also worked as postmaster during President Harrison's administration.

According to an article in the *Manassas Observer*, Baldwin built the "Baldwin House" in the 1880s and the structure went on to house several schools, including the Manassas Institute, Eastern College, Eastern College-Conservatory, a girls' school and the Swavely School, a boys' preparatory school. Finally, there were plans to make it into a vocational school, but those plans never materialized. In time, the building was deemed a safety hazard and razed and Baldwin Park put in its place. In 2015, it became the site for the Manassas Museum. There is another legacy for Isaac Baldwin. Today, Baldwin Elementary School in Manassas is named for him; its slogan is "Where Learning Is Ignited."

The Indefatigable Mr. Danzenbaker

The North American Bee-Keepers' Association held regular conventions, which gave members a chance to meet one another and share their insights and discoveries. In the President's Address (the president was A.I. Root of *Gleanings in Bee Culture*), Root spoke of difficulties overcome and the rewards of perseverance. He also spoke of Francis Danzenbaker—a man with whom he had some trouble—"but we are good friends now." Indeed, within a few

Left: Gleanings in Bee Culture (1913).

Right: L.C. Root, veteran beekeeper as well as partner, son-in-law of and co-laborer with Moses Quinby. Photographed by Edward F. Bigelow, Sound Beach, Connectivut. *Gleanings in Bee Culture* v. 40 (1912). *UMass Amherst Libraries.*

years, A.I. Root would be stocking *Danzenbaker's Facts About Bees: Management of Danzenbaker's Hive for Comb Honey*. Root also sold Danzenbaker's own style of hive components.

> *When presenting at the World's Fair in 1904, Mr. Danzenbaker, "the second greatest beekeeper in the world," gave a lengthy interview to a reporter wherein he discussed the best ways to care for and handle bees. Here are a few excerpts:*
>
> *"Stand perfectly still. Walk slowly and without waving your hands. If one of them comes at you don't duck your head or jump to one side...."*
> *The speaker is a little man, with snow-white beard and blue eyes that twinkle. One is apt to think the little man is making fun of them, because he has an amused look, but he is not, and if you are wise you will follow his instructions to the letter....*

A machine has been invented whereby foundation comb can be produced, but it must be made of pure beeswax, and it must be very thin. If it is not very thin the bees will tear it down, and if there is in it anything but pure beeswax the bees will also tear out the comb. Some people thought they would fool the bees by using paraffin in the foundation, but the bees would not be humbugged; they threw it out in a hurry.

If one should be stung by accident, bring the hand back and wip off the bee and sting together before the poison can enter the flesh. Leave the hive at once and smoke or wash off the odor of the sting, and the bees will not notice it, but if the odor is left, more and more will sting. A little smoke just as they are threatening will subdue them at once.
—St. Louis Republic, *"Francis Danzenbaker Tells How to Fight the Busy Bee" September 18, 1904*

Danzenbaker filed many patents throughout his life, including during his later years, for new hive designs, bee-smokers, bee-feeders, and packing boxes. When he passed, Root's publication got the buzz out:

Mr. Francis Danzenbaker, known as the inventor of the Danzenbaker hive, Danzenbaker section, and Danzenbaker smoker, died at Richmond, Va. on July 24, at the age of 80 years. Mr. Danzenbaker introduced to the beekeeping world the lock-cornered principle on hives—something that has been adopted by practically every beehive manufacturer in the United States. The Danzenbaker section and super are still used to a large extent. He also invented the smoker bearing his name; but as this was on the cold-blast principle it never had a very large sale. Likewise his hive, on account of the unpopularity of closed-end frames, is going out of use also. Mr. Danzenbaker was still keeping bees, and was a frequent exhibitor at various state fairs, showing his hives, honey, and bee-smoker.
—Gleanings in Bee Culture, *"Just News," September 1917*

THE GENTLE BEES

By the 1880s, Virginia beekeepers were abuzz with the possibilities of using Italian bee strains.

Italian Bee.

The Italian bee is of a striped golden color, a native of the Alps of Switzerland and North Italy. It is much hardier, energetic in its labors, and prolific than the black bee—all very valuable characteristics. Italian bees will store large quantities of surplus honey in seasons when the natives will hardly make a living. And as their queens are more prolific, they keep the stock stronger in numbers, causing the colony to winter better, enter upon its spring labors with better prospects, swarm earlier, and throw off larger swarms.

Every keeper of bees who would derive the greatest pleasure and profit from that source, should keep the Italian bee. If he is incredulous, let him obtain a single colony, and satisfy himself by experiment. He need not buy a full stock, but can obtain a fertile queen that is known to be pure, and introduce her into any colony of native bees, by first removing the black queen…The Italian queen will change the whole colony to her own kind in three or four months.

—Northern Neck News, *November 16, 1883*

According to Crane, the first Italians sent over to the United States died en route, but an American who had studied Sicilian agriculture at the request of the federal government succeeded in bringing over colonies to his nursery in New Jersey. He successfully overwintered them and began distributing Italian bees to beekeepers around the country, and they are still the favorites with many beekeepers. By the by, those early queens were able to change the colony makeup because a queen is fertilized for life on her maiden flight, which would have taken place back in Italy with Italian drones. The queens' purebred fertilized eggs would be laid once they were transplanted to America. As worker bees' lives are short and there is only one queen, the newcomers would inevitably supplant the original type, all the while being nurtured by those same native bees.

The next wave of imports, about 1880, were the Cyprians, and they really do not belong under the heading of gentle bees. Although they were very good at their work, they were also known for their vicious tempers, as were another import, the Syrian or Holy Land bees.

Other gentle bees that were tried—and are still kept—are the dark-colored Carniolan and Caucasian bees. According to the Mid-Atlantic Apiculture Research and Extension Consortium (MAAREC), the Carniolans are not as quick to breed as the Italians and are not as relaxed, but they are better at defending the hive from outsiders and are more likely to gather nectar on cooler and more overcast days. Overwintering is different for the Carniolans,

1. Dipping the Wooden Plate into melted Wax.   2. Peeling the Wax Sheet off the Wooden Plate.   3. Passing the Wax Sheet through the Foundation Machine.   4. A Sheet of Foundation fastened into a Frame, the Bees at work on it.   5. An American Apiary.   6. Uncapping the Cells.   7. Placing the Comb in the Extracting Machine.   8. Throwing the Honey out of the Comb.   9. Empty Comb ready to replace in the Hive, to be refilled with Honey by the Bees.
BEE KEEPING AND THE MANUFACTURE OF ARTIFICIAL HONEY-COMB.

Apiculture: scenes of bee-keeping and honey-gathering. Wood engraving, 1885. *Wellcome Collection. Attribution 4.0 International (CC BY 4.0).*

"The Bee-Line Home," in "Our Bee-Keeping Sisters" column. *From the* American Bee
Journal, *January 1908.*

too. Carniolans have a small number wintering over, but they produce rapid
swarms, which can be problematic if keepers are not prepared for it.

Caucasian bees have the advantage of being the friendliest bees, according
to MAAREC. At the beginning of the twentieth century, there was a push
for keeping bees in the District of Columbia, so the local newspapers would
carry stories of apian interest. This article favors the Caucasian bee:

> *The last bees brought over, and a kind whose popularity bids fair to
> make them in great demand and drive their value up to pretty stiff prices,
> is the Caucasian bee from Russia. This bee, a splendid worker and a
> very reliable citizen, is noted for the fact that though endowed with all a
> bee's physical faculties, she will not sting. At the government experiment
> stations, and at private apiaries, where she has been taken, she and her
> fellow-workers will crawl all over one's hands or face, or allow themselves
> to be handled without flying into a fury about it and using the ever-ready
> sting as the German bee will invariably do. It is expected that pure strains
> of Caucasian will be introduced as rapidly as possible and so cause a*

greater spread of the beekeeping industry, since the most objectionable
features, that of contending with belligerent bees, will be removed.
—*The* Washington Herald, *July 16, 1907*

The Caucasian bees are still relatively rare compared to the Italian, possibly because they make quite a bit more propolis, which makes producing comb honey for sale more difficult, although newer strains may be less likely to do this.

Hybrid bees, some informally done and some carrying brand names such as Midnite and Starline, are produced by crossing different strains, can keep some of the best qualities of each parent type, mating a virgin queen of one type with a drone of another, until that population is stabilized and becomes its own type.

Because climatic conditions vary from location to location, even within the state, which runs the gamut from Tidewater to the Highlands, it is usually advised that would-be beekeepers buy their stock from local beekeepers with good reputations for the best chance of success.

Understandably, however gentle the bees, protective clothing is always a wise investment.

FEISTY SWARMS

What about "killer bees"? Bees that produce honey and are good at protecting their brood, hive home, stash of honey and each other have earned the nickname "killer bees."

The Western honeybee (as opposed to types in Asia, for example) is *Apis mellifera*—*Apis* for "bee" and *mellifera* for "honey-bearer." The feisty variety that lives in tropical Africa—and now in many tropical regions—is named *Apis mellifera scutellata*, as opposed to *Apis mellifera ligustica* (Italian honeybee) or *Apis mellifera mellifera* (European dark bee), that immigrant to Jamestown and elsewhere that kept colonial and early American honey jars filled.

The "Africanized honeybees" were first brought to Brazil in 1956. As the insects were accustomed to tropical regions on the African continent, it was reasoned they would do well on a new environment with similar conditions. They did well. Very well. So well, in fact, that by 1986, according to Crane, they had taken over most of South and Central America, displacing the European honeybees that had been brought in to supplement the stingless but less productive native bee. The original thought of Dr. Warwick Kerr, the researcher who imported them, was to cross his imported species with gentler ones to get the best of both traits. It was an admirable idea, but the bees swarmed, as they will; escaped the lab; and made their way into the countryside. The rest is history and resulted in some shiver-worthy B movies, better protective clothing and something new for U.S. entomologists to worry about. According to an article in the December 13, 1990 issue of the *Recorder*, a "pioneering swarm" was caught in a trap in October of that year in Hidalgo, Texas. But they were not the last.

Africanized bees made their way readily to tropical areas in the United States, such as Florida, but were they ever in Virginia? Yes.

According to an article that appeared in the *Southside Sentinel* on July 27, 2000, Africanized honeybees had at last been found in Virginia. USDA scientists used a computer-assisted program to identify the bees, which look much as other bees, as they intermingle. Though they looked like native honeybees, the goat they managed to attack and kill in Low Moor, located near the mountains, was sufficiently suspicious to have the authorities investigate further. It was noted in a contemporaneous *Washington Post* article that four people were badly stung as well and were sent to the hospital. Near the site of the attack, there were two swarms and a hive. Inside were the European honeybees, while outside, ready to wage war, were the interlopers. Not being certain of the bees' identities at that time, both swarms were destroyed. It was thought that the incomers were an isolated swarm that had caught a ride from the south on a truck or a rail car.

FOOL'S GOLD, OR HUCKSTER'S HONEY

Where there's money to be made, there's money to be stolen. Bees are honest if sometimes irascible workers, but some humans who sold their treasure were not always as virtuous.

Hive honey is a mixture of glucose and fructose and similar in sweetness to sucrose—standard sugar. It is time-consuming for the bees to make (and the keepers to harvest) and is therefore pricey. If a fellow could find a way to produce something that would trick a city-dweller's palate and make a more generous profit, what, he might be thinking to himself, would be the harm?

According to Crane, by the 1860s, some "honey" on the American market was thinned out with glucose—made from potatoes and imported from Europe. Early on, Americans, such as Virginian Landon Carter, had tried to make a crude form of corn syrup, but by the 1870s, corn-based glucose was being successfully manufactured and marketed—and slipped into jars labeled honey. This began happening just about the same time that genuine extracted honey was coming on the market. Customers got wind of the corn syrup switch, which made them quite reluctant to put their money down for extracted honey, which looked much the same, perhaps even a bit better, as true honey tends to crystallize after it's been stored for a while.

Bee experts, such as Moses Quinby, tried to educate the public that a common tactic used by these charlatans was to place a piece of old comb in a jelly cup and fill the rest up with glucose, its shining clarity belying its false nature. Honest beekeepers gathered signatures for Congress to do something, to no avail.

The formulas for faking honey were many and varied. C. Loomis recounts in his article "Some Lore of Yankee Genius, 1831–1863" another way of stretching the honey harvest without the addition of imported European ingredients:

MOLASSES HONEY
A new edition of wooden nutmegs in the shape of molasses honey, has, of late, formed quite a "notion" for "the trade." It is principally sold by peddlers and is made by adding ten gallons of sugar-house molasses, three of water and two of good honey, and boiling them together. This honey sells from eight to twelve and a half cents a pound, and the water is "dog cheap." The honey generally takes the name of "Southern honey," and is probably rightly named, so far as the molasses part is concerned.

Harvey Wiley, later dubbed the "Father of the FDA," began life on a farm. After serving in the Union army during the Civil War, he changed his career ambitions from medicine to chemistry, eventually becoming the state chemist for Indiana. As part of his duties, he analyzed various sweeteners and syrups available for sale in his state, natural and man-made. He discovered many of the products, such as honey and maple syrup, were not what they should be. One product, though entirely glucose, appeared similar to expensive white clover honey and could be profitably sold at half the price of the real article, which meant there was no profit to be had for true honey selling in the same market. Wiley was hired by the USDA, where he went on to do impressive things.

The Pure Food and Drugs Act of 1906 gave Wiley the muscle he needed to change the industry with a court case featuring a product advertised as "pure strained honey" and sold from Philadelphia to the Detroit market turned out to contain glucose. With the new law in place, it was an actionable case.

Smaller "producers" had their ways of getting an unearned profit as well. In the September 1, 1983 issue of the *Mountain Laurel*, Adam Clement of Ararat, Virginia, was featured as a local craftsman. Born on July 3, 1901, he had kept bees since the 1930s, having been taught by his mother—and he, in turn, had taught his son. He remembered some tricks of trade others had used:

> He said occasionally people boil sugar water with alum which creates a syrup. They will then place a section or two of comb in a jar and fill it with the syrup. This way, a little bit of honey will go a long way but the result is no more than honey flavored sugar water that looks like clear honey. But he, at 82, was determined to "sell it like I get it."

Here's a bit more, from the same issue, on how he worked with the produce of his twenty-five to thirty hives:

> His ways are old fashioned, even the way he separates the wax. In his backyard in the shade of ancient trees, he melts the wax in an old black pot over an open fire. He sells bees wax in large blocks, along with honey.

Of course, there was another kind of cheat, the unscrupulous dealer. Many a farmer who produced more honey than his local market could sell would ship the product to professional dealers, often in the north, via railway. Often a dishonest dealer would get the better of the farmer, but there were times when the farmer triumphed:

HOW A VIRGINIAN GOT AHEAD OF A YORK COUNTY SCAMP.
From the Berryville (Va.) Courier

Recently Mr. H.P. Deahl, of Berryville, sold to a merchant in York, Pa., about five hundred pounds of honey. Instead of receiving a check Mr. Deahl received a letter from the merchant's son saying the honey was almost worthless and would be sold for what it would bring. Mr. Deahl promptly took a train for York and dropped into the store he had shipped to. Upon inquiry he found that he was in the presence of the young man who had written the letter which took him to York, and he asked if he had any honey for sale.

"Oh, yes," was the reply, "I have a fine article just from Virginia, and will show you a sample of it," and thereupon stepped back and in a few minutes returned with some of the beautiful honey. "Is it all like this?" asked Mr. Deahl. "Yes, sir," said the young man. "How much have you?" Deahl next asked. "About 500 pounds." "Are you sure the lot is as good as that?" he next asked, "as I am a good judge of honey." "Just walk back here and see for yourself," said the young man. "Well, I'm glad to hear you say so," said Mr. Deahl. "And now I'll introduce myself. I am Mr. Deahl, to whom you penned this letter"—producing the letter—"and the next time you undertake to play a sharp game be sure of your man first." If a thunderbolt had shaken the house the young man could not have been more startled at the manner he was confronted by the person he sought to victimize with rascality, and he was compelled to hang his head in shame. Mr. Deahl demanded his money and after a few words a check for it was issued.
—Shenandoah Herald, *February 11, 1887*

Less-than-honest honey has continued to be a problem. In January 1986, the *Rappahannock Record* announced that the Virginia Department of Agriculture and Consumer Services (VDACS), in cooperation with Virginia honey producers and beekeepers, had put out its first Virginia honey guide. The publication listed honey producers, details on Virginia honey and where to get beekeeping supplies. The article also included words of warning from Glynn Moreland, VDACS direct marketing agent: "Finding pure Virginia honey is not a simple as it would seem. High fructose syrup is sometimes marketed as honey, and much of the honey on the market is imported from Mexico and China which creates a situation where local producers sell their honey to the government on the price support program. Thus, much of the Virginia honey is not available to the consumer."

READ ALL ABOUT IT

Getting the Latest Buzz in Local Newspapers

While specialty publications, such as the *American Bee Journal* and *Gleanings in Bee Culture*, supplied one audience with apiarian education, local newspapers provided tips to everyone in their readership. Horoscopes and crosswords might not have been plentiful in the late nineteenth and early twentieth centuries, but columns touching on the basics of farming were widespread, taking the approach of the farmers' friend.

A lot of these stories were reprinted from city to city, and eventually, they were shared contractually as syndicated columns, following the rule printing "fresh" copy at the same time across the country so that everyone, from Florida to Maine to California, might have read the same story at the same time. Before network news gave us all a sense of common knowledge, these columns accomplished something similar without the cameras and commercial breaks.

FARMER'S FRIEND COLUMNS

The *Richmond Planet* (1889–1930), a renowned African American newspaper, ran columns on poultry and bees regularly, sometimes reprinted from other sources. For example, an article on "Handling Comb Honey," appearing

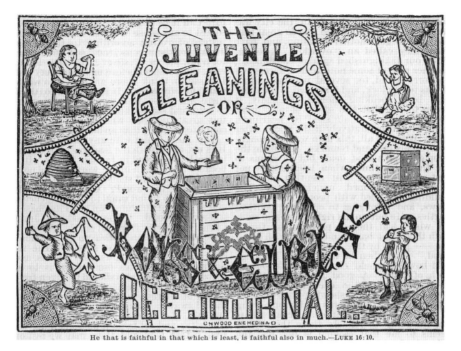

"The Juvenile Gleanings, or Boys' & Girls' Bee Journal." *From* Gleanings in Bee Culture, *January 1884.*

in the January 23, 1904 issue, was first printed in a publication called *Orange Judd Farmer*. Orange Judd, for that was the publisher's name, was an American who had philosophy similar to that of seventeenth-century scholar Samuel Hartlib. Judd wanted to find a way to bring the latest in scientific advancements to farmers, and the rise of serial publications in the nineteenth century suited his purpose. The *Richmond Planet* also reprinted "Notes on Keeping Bees Through Winter," from *Orange Judd Farmer* and tapped *Gleanings in Bee Culture* for an article on "Raspberries for Honey," among its many useful articles.

Besides the care of the bees, newspapers advised on how to best market their product. The December 1, 1911 issue of the *Recorder* ran a column on "Hum of the Hive," which offered simple yet useful invectives such as packaging the honey as attractively as possible (with examples of how to do this) and using a honey extractor to save the bees' time at making fresh comb—allowing them to focus on fresh honey production instead. The article also gave encouraging words on the honey and wax market, helping would-be beekeepers envision success.

Left: People posed on porch of the *Planet* newspaper publishing house, Richmond, Virginia. *African American Photographs Assembled for 1900 Paris Exposition; Library of Congress.*

Right: "Self-made Men of Our Times—Orange Judd, Esq. of *The American Agriculturalist*." *Chimney Corner* (1870–73).

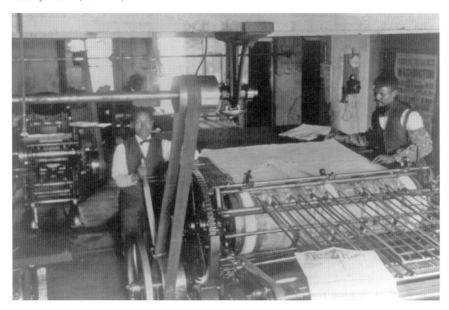

Press room of the *Planet* newspaper, Richmond, Virginia, 1899. *African American Photographs Assembled for 1900 Paris Exposition; Library of Congress.*

The *Peninsula Enterprise* shared these words of wisdom in its August 27, 1910 issue. Use the advice only after consulting a modern, experienced beekeeper, please.

Beekeepers, Attention!
Be sure to wash your hands and face in vinegar before you try to rob the bees.
When you want to take out honey, cut out all the white and leave the dark for the bees.
Bees will make just as much honey in a box hive as they would in a costly patented one.
Sprinkle salt under and around your hive to keep away the moths, the enemies of the bees.
The bee's business end strikes everyone forcibly.
No product now wasted can be more easily saved than nectar which bees work up into honey.
The question is frequently asked why extract honey is sold cheaper than comb honey. It is because the comb is of more value than the honey. It requires twenty pounds of honey to make one pound of comb.
To hive bees when they swarm throw water on them while they are swarming, and they will not leave or settle high. If it is a large limb they settle on, saw it off and let it fall on a sheet, then sprinkle them with water, so they won't swarm again, and poor [sic] them in the hive and let them set until dark.

HOME ECONOMICS

The United States had many more small farms in the past than the present, and beehives were very desirable—and their harvest so useful. Families and individuals who did not live on farms were also encouraged to keep bees by magazines. And what to do with all that honey and wax? The magazines had answers for that, too.

Various Uses of Extracted Honey.

The avenues for the consumption of extracted honey are many, and daily increasing. Among the more common, American Bee Journal *cites the following: table use, confectionery, pastry and cakes, jellies and jams;*

Top: American Homes and Gardens, February 1912 issue. The article discusses the resurgence in bee popularity as a popular "outdoor activity for after business hours." They recommend Italian bees for their sweeter tempers.

Bottom: "Questions and Answers with Dr. C.C. Miller." *American Bee Journal*, 1900.

canning and preserving fruit, both cooked and in its natural state; curing hams and meats of various kinds, in making mead, metheglin, honey wines, harvest drinks and liquors; honey vinegar, honey egg foam, medicinal preparations, sirups, ointments and salves. It forms the principal ingredient in the formation of printers' rollers, and is used in the manufacture of beer, ale and tobacco.
—Roanoke Daily Times, *March 1, 1890*

An 1883 issue of the *Peninsula Enterprise* had suggestions for how beeswax could help with housecleaning:

THINGS NOT KNOWN.—
*That beeswax and salt will make your rusty flat-irons as clean and as smooth as glass. Tie of lump of wax in a rag and keep it for that purpose. When the irons are hot, rub them first with the wax rag, then scour them with a paper or cloth sprinkled with salt. —*Hall's Journal of Health
GRAFTING WAX.—A reader writes to us for a recipe for making grafting wax that will not melt in the summer nor crack in the winter. Replying, we would say that three parts resin, three parts beeswax and two parts tallow will make an excellent grafting wax (for gardeners).

FIG. 14.—KOLB & GROBER STEAM WAX-PRESS

Kolb & Grober Steam Wax-Press, *Gleanings in Bee Culture*, 1901.

Families learned in a 1908 issue of *Virginia Farmer* that beeswax, coupled with tallow (rendered animal fat) and kerosene (handy already for lamps) could be used to waterproof moccasins. A 1922 issue of the *Norfolk Post* gave a recipe for making "the best wax for a floor," which combined beeswax with paraffin and turpentine. The family mechanic learned in the *Recorder's* You Auto Know column in 1921 that "to prevent trouble when driving screws into hard wood apply beeswax to the screw, thereby relieving the friction."

The *Norfolk Post's* "Spare Time Jobs" column in 1922 had a suggestion for folks who were making do with old furniture:

> *When cracks appear in furniture it is a common custom to fill them up with putty. Then, folks who do it, find that putty cracks and makes the crevices look almost as bad as in the first place.*
>
> *The next time try beeswax. This will fill up the cracks and hold its form. You can wash or varnish over it. Careful varnishing over beeswax-filled cracks will hide the cracks completely.*

Another 1922 issue of the same paper had something for the children's benefit:

When the little folks get out in the rain with boots on, water sometimes seeps in at the seams. You can make these waterproof by using a mixture of equal parts of mutton fat, beeswax, and sweet oil. Put this on the stove until it is well blended. Then let it cool. Apply on the boots, particularly where they are seamed and at the place where the soles and uppers come together.

COMMUNITY NEWS

With bees abounding and given to swarming, sometimes they were the story, especially in otherwise sleepy country neighborhoods. On March 9, 1893, the *Bedford Democrat* reported:

> *FROM PENICKS*
> *We had the severest wind-storm in this section that has been here for some time, it overturned one of your scribe's best beehives and broke up twenty-five pounds of nice honey. It is rough on the bees, but means a sweet tooth for me… —OBSERVER*

Before the time of the automobile, the blacksmith was the mechanic. On June 7, 1902, the *Virginia* noted a change in the local smith's daily routine:

> *Ewell, VA., June 5*
> *Mr. St. John captured a swarm of bees which had settled down just back of his blacksmith shop Tuesday. Where they came from he has no idea.*

The blacksmith picked up the stray swarm handily enough, but sometimes it was up to the law to manage trespassing honeybees:

> *Sheriff Hives Bees*
>
> *MONTEREY—A swarm of runaway honeybees clustered in the branches of a locust tree on the courthouse lawn Tuesday but were soon hived by Sheriff Bird, who climbed the tree, cut off the limb, and lowered it to the ground with a wire.*
> *—The* Recorder, *June 18, 1920*

These bees made house calls:

Not Only Gets Honey but Also Swarm of Bees

When Dr. S.C. Dickinson of Lakeview Heights brought home a bucket filled with honey and honeycombs, he had no idea that he was at the same time transporting a hive of honeybees. But Sunday morning when he took the lid off the bucket he was amazed to be met with hundreds of the buzzing workers seeking a place to swarm.

Search among the bees for their queen failed to reveal one and so it is thought the hive will die as they will only be drones with their queen which evidently was left in the tree from which the doctor got his honey.

—Suffolk News-Herald, *June 17, 1929*

Not everyone was so sanguine about bees buzzing around the neighborhood. In a letter to the editor of the *Roanoke Times*, the "Bee Man" hotly defended the winged ones from the slander of "The Kicker," who was not best pleased with honeybees on the loose:

SAYS IT'S A GOOD SIGN

To the Editor of the Times: Referring to the communication of "The Kicker" in The Times *of this morning, wherein he complains that Roanoke is infested with honey bees, permit me to say that this is a good sign. Wherever civilization has established itself the honey bee has always followed. Of course if a community is barbarous, heathenish and uncivilized, there will be no honey bees to trouble the people; but whenever we attain to the high standard now enjoyed by the people of Roanoke we should indeed feel slighted if we were ignored by the honey bee. As to the "Kicker," like the poor, he is with us always.*

But seriously, Mr. Editor, the complaint made by "The Kicker" is a very foolish one to lay before the public. Most of our citizens, fortunately, have in their time been country people, and they know something of the "pest" referred to. But I doubt if there are a dozen beehives in all the city of Roanoke, unless they be on the extreme outskirts of the city.

Now whoever heard of honey bees attacking and destroying crops of peaches plums and other fruits? The honey bee never touches fruit of any kind unless it be first bruised or injured by decay or is being prepared for use. The complaint of "Kicker" is certainly a silly one; but the idea he puts forth as to placing a prohibitory license on the bee keeper is bright and

unique. Let the council give him a premium for the suggestion, though the idea of taxing a thing out of existence is not a new one, and it might with profit be extended to the average kicker. THE BEE MAN.
Roanoke, August 6, 1897.

As of this writing, the statue of General Robert E. Lee in Richmond has been removed. But more than one hundred years ago, it was still on what was then called Monument Avenue—and, as some sharp-eyed onlookers noticed—doing double-duty as a beehive:

LEE STATUE A BEE HIVE
Horse and Rider Probably Contain a Goodly Quantity of Honey.

The interesting discovery was made yesterday that the Lee equestrian statue in the western part of the city is the home of a large number of honeybees, and probably contains a goodly quantity of the delicious provisions which have been industriously stored up for the coming winter.

For some time bees have been noticed in considerable numbers about the small openings at the mouth and nostrils of the horse and the mouth of the rider. More than once considerable swarms have come out of these openings which are believed to be the only openings to the interior of the statue. When it is remembered that the statue of both horse and rider is merely a shell less than a half-inch thick it will be at once seen what a commodious and comfortable home and retreat for honey-gatherers the interior of the statue provides.

It is not known whether the openings to the statue are large enough to allow sparrows to enter. If so, the statue is probably partially full of the trash which they collect to make their nests. As sparrows can get through a wonderfully small opening, this is quite possible but no sparrows or other small birds have been noticed going in or out of the statue as has been the case with the bees. The latter have certainly found a safe place for gathering their winter's supplies and one in which they will not and cannot be molested. It will give an added interest to the many who visit it, to know that it is probably well filled with honey of the best make and reputation.
—The Times, *October 2, 1901*

Harold John Goyne Sr. (1886–1982) of Chester, in Chesterfield County, near Richmond—also known as "Harry" and "Honeybee"—was asked by reporters to give his opinion of the occupied statue's contents, as he was a well-known beekeeper, in a follow-up story in 1932. Goyne relayed that the statue had been an occupied hive for nearly two decades "or perhaps longer." (Almost certainly longer as the 1901 story attests.) A 1936 report in the *Richmond Times-Dispatch* noted that the bees had moved on.

Goyne and his kin had more staying power. Born in Pennsylvania, he spent much of his adult life in the environs of Richmond. In 1915, he advertised in the *Richmond Times-Dispatch* that he had won nine first-place prizes at the State Fair—and was a winner for the fourth year running. Further, he would be at the Great Southside Virginia Fair and have "Combed Honey, Strained Honey, Beeswax, Bee Hives, and Supplies" for sale. Visitors would also have an opportunity to "watch the bees at work," presumably in an observation hive.

"Honeybee" Goyne passed on a love of beekeeping to his son "Junie," also known as Harry J. Goyne Jr. (1917–2006), the eldest of his six children. Junie studied honeybees at the University of North Carolina's extension office and received a master beekeepers' certification, a program extension agencies in many states, including Virginia, continue today. Master beekeepers, and Junie Goyne was no exception, share their knowledge with less experienced beekeepers. Readers can learn more about the program at https://www. virginiabeekeepers.org/Master-Beekeeper-Program.

FIELDS (AND HIVES) OF GOLD

The twentieth century ushered in a rush of liquid gold for those committed to beekeeping on a larger scale, as noted in the *Staunton Spectator and Vindicator*, on May 19, 1905:

MAKING MONEY WITH BEES
The Bee Industry Has Grown Amazingly During the Last Twenty Years.

Few city people realize that apiculture has developed into a practical money-making industry during the last 20 years, until now the average amount of honey put on the market each year is upward of 100,000,000 pounds, representing a money value of from $8,000,000 to $10,000,000.

In a favorable locality, one hive, with its average colony of 35,000 workers and a queen, will turn out from 30 to 40 pounds of honey, besides the 15 or 20 necessary to feed the hive through the winter.

A few hives, in any ordinary country district, should each bring in a clear two dollars a year profit at the lowest estimate. On a poultry and fruit farm where clover, sunflower and millet are grown for the poultry the yield of honey should be much larger if the apiary is restricted to 20 or 30 hives.

However, conditions varied, and farmers in deforested areas were not having an easy time of it. This gentleman went for the personal touch, as described in a Poultry & Bees column that ran in the *Tazewell Republican* in 1898:

A Sweet History

Disposing of Honey
How One Beekeeper Managed to Do It with Decidedly Gratifying
Financial Results

How to dispose of the honey crop profitably is becoming a serious problem with most bee-keepers. Not many years ago it was easy to raise comb honey, says H.D. Burrell in Bee Culture. Ship it to some commission house in a near-by city and realize 16 to 20 cents a pound on it. Now in many places most of the honey-producing timber is gone, and waste lands reclaimed and cultivated. These causes, with frequent poor seasons, render the honey crop uncertain; and, worst of all, comb honey in the cities is quoted 7 to 12 cents.

Formerly I raised comb honey almost exclusively and shipped nearly all of it to commission houses. But some years ago I unexpectedly had about a ton of autumn-extracted honey to dispose of. Shipped to a commission house it would probably have netted four to five cents a pound some time. I had never tried peddling honey, and was very much prejudiced against peddlers and peddling; but I wanted more for that honey. I loaded some of it into the wagon, put up in convenient packages for retailing and started, though with much trepidation. I knew a few rebuffs would send that honey to the city for what it would bring. But I sold honey at nearly every house, over 300 pounds the first day, and decided that peddling (honey at least) was not such bad business after all. Many neighbors and acquaintances who had passed by frequently for years and seen the sign: "Honey for Sale," but never bought a pound of my honey, bought freely when it was carried to them. And they didn't buy afterward, either, unless I carried it to them and asked them to buy.

The ton of honey was soon sold at eight to eleven cents per pound, according to quantity wanted, and several thousand pounds more were bought and sold at a fair profit. Since that time I have raised mostly extracted honey, always retail it myself, and am getting the same prices now in these times of very low prices that I did ten years ago. Honey, if a good article, will sell itself almost anywhere, if given a fair chance. I have never found a place, in country or town, where it would not sell fairly well any time of the year, though in the fall is best in my experience, after the bulk of the fruit is gone and the many needs of the winter season have not yet taxed the pocketbook.

THE EDUCATED FARMER

Besides farmers' groups, bee societies, magazines and newspaper columns, as the nineteenth century closed, there arose another route for young students to learn about the agricultural sciences. In addition to the traditional colleges and universities, which taught students who came to them, usually already with a background in Latin and Greek, there arose both normal schools and polytechnical institutes. The former, active from about the 1880s to the 1920s and 1930s, emphasized teacher education, their name being drawn from the French teacher-training schools, the *école normale*, first begun in 1685 by the Brothers of Christian Schools to create a standard for teacher education.

There was a great need for teachers, as attendance at public schools was exploding in the wake of the Civil War and the waves of immigration. Typically, education at a normal school would last six weeks to a few months. Current Virginia colleges and universities that transitioned from their beginnings as normal schools include: University of Mary Washington, Longwood University, James Madison University and Radford University, whose symbol is a beehive.

James Madison University recently began a student club, the Bee Friendly Beekeepers, which manages two hives on campus. It is also part of the Bee Campus USA program, which, in conjunction with Bee USA, encourages communities to help sustain pollinators in their plantings. Randolph College, in Lynchburg, and the University of Richmond have also joined the program.

Land-grant schools—which might also be known as land-grant colleges, land-grant universities or land-grant institutions—were initially funded under the Morrill Acts of 1862 and 1890 to allow states to sell or use federally controlled land they were given (granted) to start schools whose mission would be focus on the teaching of practical agriculture, science, military science and engineering (though "without excluding...classical studies"). Virginia Polytechnic and State University (Virginia Tech) and Virginia State University in Hampton began as land-grant colleges. Today, Virginia Tech is home to the Virginia Cooperative Extension Agency, which administers the Master Beekeeper program.

Sometimes technical schools and normal schools were combined into one institution, as in the case of Virginia Normal and Industrial Institute in Hampton, which began as Virginia Normal and Collegiate Institute and eventually became Virginia State University in 1979. This school offered

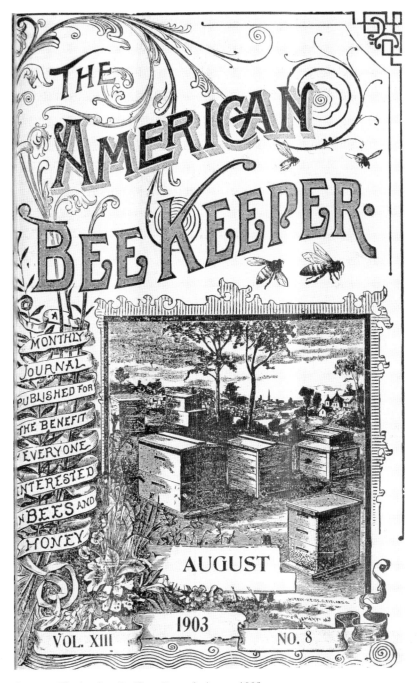

Cover to *The American Bee Keeper* 8, no. 8, August 1903.

Bee Culture was a two-month course that met five periods per week. Photo of the Hampton Institute, Virginia Plant Study Lab, 1899. *Library of Congress.*

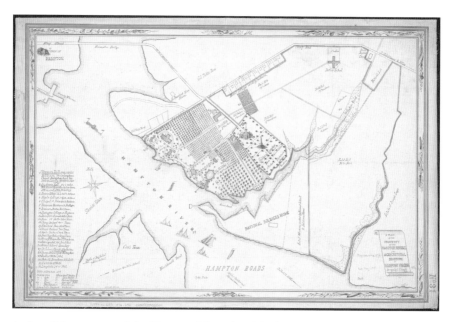

A plan of the property of the Hampton Normal and Agricultural Institute at Hampton, Virginia. *Semple, F. A. Publisher: American Photo-Lithographic Company Date: 1876.*

beekeeping as on its courses in the early years. Today, VSU hosts beekeeping classes as part of its small farm educational outreach program. Recent classes have been taught by VDACS (Virginia Department of Agriculture and Consumer Services) state apiarist Keith Tignor.

The Government Takes Notice

The U.S. Patent Office began publishing reports on apiculture in the 1850s. The Department of Agriculture was established in 1862 by President Abraham Lincoln, who called it "The People's Department," understandably, since so many citizens were farmers. The USDA took up the task of publishing bee reports, but things would take a decidedly scientific turn when Everett Franklin Phillips (1878–1951) took the reins as commissioner in 1905. The new commissioner had a doctorate in biology and a determination to add the benefits of modern science to apiculture.

Forest Insect Investigations, Washington, D.C. *Left to right*: W.F. Fiske, Phillips and Jesse L. Webb. *USDA Forest Service, Region 6, State and Private Forestry, Forest Health Protection; public domain.*

He established the Bee Culture Laboratory in the D.C. suburbs and tasked it with studying bee diseases such as foul brood, the best ways to overwinter and more.

It was Dr. Phillips who appealed to Congress in 1922 to stop unsupervised (without USDA approval) importations of bees, an action triggered by the devastating effects of Isle of Wight Disease (IoWD or Acarine), believed to be caused by *Acarapis woodi* mites living and reproducing in the bees' tracheae. Later it was found that *Acarine* was a co-morbidity with chronic bee paralysis virus (CBPV), which was the main culprit. It was a truly devastating disease, first reported in 1904 on Britain's Isle of Wight. It wiped out most of the native bee population of the British Isles, and Dr. Phillips was determined to not have it here. Fortunately, Brother Adam (1898–1996), beekeeper at Buckfast Abbey, a Benedictine monastery in Devonshire, England, developed the Buckfast bee, which seems to be immune to the effects of the virus. The Buckfast bee, a careful blending of European dark or black bees and Italian bees, is now being bred around the world and can be acquired in Virginia.

Dr. Phillips was also interested in raising the annual honey crop, at that time about 250 million pounds per year. To do this, he wanted to increase the number of skilled commercial beekeepers—and introduce beekeeping into more communities. On the heels of the First World War, he also suggested that beekeeping would be a good occupation for veterans returning from war.

By 1924, Dr. Phillips was done with Washington bureaucracy and moved to Ithaca, New York, where he taught apiculture at Cornell University, both to students and local beekeepers; campaigned for federal inspection of

Beekeeping Instruction for Injured Soldiers. Harris & Ewing, photographer, 1918. *Library of Congress.*

"Overcoats for Bees the Latest," Bee Culture Laboratory at the National Agricultural Research Center, Beltsville, Maryland, 1939. *Library of Congress.*

apiaries and promoted cooperative extension programs in apiculture. The E.F. Phillips Beekeeping Collection, housed at the A.R. Mann Library at Cornell University, is today one of the largest beekeeping libraries in the world, containing some of the oldest existing beekeeping treatises, as well as current publications.

Scientific work on bees continued at both the state and federal level, but besides the science, there were other ways the government supported the honey crop. The Farm Service Agency of the USDA has provided loans to commercial beekeepers through its Honey Program, both for marketing (MALs) and loan deficiency payments (LDP).

For beekeepers on a smaller scale, the State of Virginia runs a program to provide beekeeping equipment to interested citizens, at least in part due to fears that the honeybees wouldn't recover on their own after a long run of CCD (colony collapse disorder). In CCD, worker bees abandon what seems to be an otherwise well-functioning hive and its queen, nurse bees and food supply.

Suggestions for what causes CCD are numerous, from mites to genetics, but two beekeepers this author spoke to believed it was pesticides confusing the delicate senses of the worker bees, who could no longer find their way home. As pesticides are used on most large-scale farms, a state initiative, VDACS' Pollinator Protection Plan, enables better communication between beekeepers and farmers who may be spraying pesticides.

Honeybees on the Homefront

In the May 21, 1917 issue of the *Richmond Times-Dispatch*, Virginia beekeepers were alerted to a potential rush on their market:

FACTS FOR VIRGINIA FARMERS

BLACKSBURG, VA. May 20,—W.J. Schoene, State entomologist, has this to say to the bee keepers of Virginia:

This is the year that the bee keepers should recover the losses that they sustained last season because of unfavorable weather. There will probably be a shortage of sugar in the United States in the near future, and there will be need for all the honey that can be produced. This offers an opportunity to the bee keeper to extend his business in such a way as to make it of lasting benefit to himself, while he is at the same time doing a patriotic duty. It is, therefore, suggested and urged that you increase your apiary as much as is consistent with getting a fair crop per colony, and especially that you manipulate the bees so as to obtain maximum yields.

It has been learned by corresponding with several hundred bee keepers in this State that fully 50 per cent of the bee keepers experience some kind of difficulty with their bees. There has been a good many complaints about moths, and from some localities "disease" has been reported. Also a number of persons have lost some of their colonies because they were unable to control swarming. These and many other troubles can be greatly reduced or avoided by the use of modern hives and proper understanding of the principles of bee culture.

As a rule, bees in box hives produce for the bee keeper about ten pounds per colony, whereas, bees in movable frame hives, properly managed, will average fifty to 100 pounds of comb honey in the same season. There are a number of bulletins available for free distribution which tell how to transfer bees and how they should be managed to secure the greatest amount of honey.

Even where people have only one or two colonies of bees, these should produce a quantity of table honey and, in addition, a surplus for cooking. Owing to the high price of sugar, persons having only a few colonies of bees should take pains to see that these are in condition to gather the nectar during the time of honey flow.

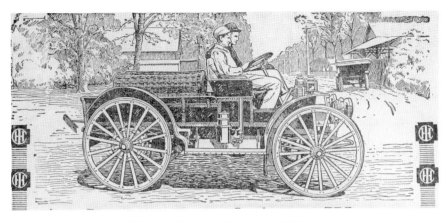

"The International Auto Wagon," *Gleanings in Bee Culture*, 1912.

W.J. Schoene was right on the money when it came to upcoming sugar shortages, and hopefully the paper's subscribers took heed, as just over a month had passed since Congress voted to declare war on Germany.

Shortly after the war began, the recently formed U.S. Food Administration pushed Americans to use less sugar and other foods needed by American forces and allies. As was to be expected, Dr. Phillips gathered beekeepers at a meeting to produce more honey, and the Extension Service (which now runs the Master Beekeeper program) sent employees around the country to teach best beekeeping practices. Other agencies did their bit to help the beekeepers—the U.S. Fuel Administration let factories making beekeeping supplies run on "fuelless days," and the U.S. Postal Service allowed bees to be shipped by parcel post.

In March of the following year, the *Times-Dispatch* sponsored a contest in its children's section and invited essays on how the war was affecting the homefront. Young Sadie Dunnavant wrote, in part:

> *We should save food because in the future food may be more scarce, and we must feed our soldiers and allies so they can win the war.*
>
> *We can save by substituting and by not being wasteful....We can substitute honey and syrups for sugar, potatoes, rice, barley and corn for wheat, eggs, fish and oysters for meats and poultry fats and vegetable fats for animal fats.*
>
> *If we do not save food the Germans may win the war, and we will be under the Kaiser's rule and will not have a president.*
> —Richmond Times-Dispatch, *March 24, 1918*

Newspapers published practical substitutes for most-wanted goods, including honey for sugar. The July 24, 2018 issue of *World News* advised housewives that cherries could be canned with "honey and other syrups" in place of sugar syrup.

After the Great War, bees weren't ready to be downsized. Again, education was the key to success:

Study Beekeeping Under Vocational Education Board.

Before sugar was made in quantities from cane for commercial purposes much of the sweet in food came from honey. Shortage of sugar during the war restored honey to its former popularity, and this increased demand served, as it usually does, to raise the price. For these reasons, the production of honey promises to be a profitable business.

The federal board for vocational education encourages the disabled soldier who has a leaning toward outdoor life and who wants independence to take up the subject of beekeeping. The work is light and the hours short. The investment requires little money but a large amount of brains, and the financial returns are good.
—Evening Star *(Washington, D.C.), September 3, 1919*

The Second World War saw a return to rationing and another rise in the need for honey as a substitute for sugar. Beeswax, too, was valued, as it could be used as a protective coating for munitions and canvas goods, and Congress correspondingly added more money to the bee-culture budget.

After that war, there was still a need for more bees as men returned to the fields and factories, ready to work and ready to eat. The country needed its pollinators and was already concerned about the effects of toxic crop treatments.

Uncle Sam in Need of More Bees

To aid in providing more adequate pollination of legume forage crops, fruits and vegetables, the U.S. Department of Agriculture has included in this year's Goals Program a proposal that the colonies of bees in this country be increased by 8 percent.

Bees are old friends of mankind. What may prove to be man's most ancient work of art, a pre-historic painting in red found in a cave near Valencia, Spain, and supposed to be about 15,000 years old, shows a man surrounded by bees taking honey combs out of a hole in a cliff to place in a basket. Ever since, man has been enjoying this natural sweet, and the by-product, beeswax. Today, the activity of the bees as pollinating agents is considered to have a value conservatively estimated at 10 to 20 times the value of the honey and beeswax they produce. Bumblebees and other former pollinating insects have been decreasing rapidly as a result of poisonous sprays and dusts, and from the clean cultivation that has destroyed many of their homes—thus placing a greater pollinating burden on the honeybees. At least 50 crops depend upon bees for pollination or yield more abundantly when bees are working.

The proposed goal of 8 per cent increase in the number of colonies of bees has been broken down by the Department into a specific goal figure for each State, according to its individual needs for building up legume seed production, fruit output, etc. For effective economy, most States should have even more colonies of bees than the proposed goals.

—Virginia Farm Bureau News, *March 1, 1946*

HONEYBEES' FORTUNES
EBB AND FLOW

In 2018, the Eastern Apicultural Society of North America held its conference in Virginia. Not surprisingly, "Where It All Began," an article in its after-conference report in its *Journal of the Eastern Apicultural Society of North America*, mentions the skeps that could be seen in colonial Jamestown's living museum. This event coincided with the 100th anniversary of the Virginia State Beekeepers' Association, and its local association members were naturally in attendance. They remarked that Virginia's most common honey was wildflower, but specialty honeys, such as mountain-gathered sourwood, were favorites, as well as honeys made from linden and basswood trees. The after-conference report also noted that most Virginia beekeepers were small in scale, keeping hives as a sideline, with new keepers emerging from classes taught by the state extension agents or local associations and keepers every year.

The tone of the 2018 article was upbeat, but some years have not been so golden. For example, all it takes is a cold lingering winter for a setback, as the state's beekeepers experienced in 1949. But George H. Rea, a bee man from Virginia Tech, had a helpful suggestion for how to help hungry bees:

> *Virginia's honey bees are in a bad way this spring.*
> *They have found the damp, cool weather not to their liking for flights, with the result that many of them are staying at home and starving to death.*
> *George H. Rea, newly appointed Extension bee specialist at V.P.I., says he has found many colonies dead or starving; and that, in general, they are*

too weak to work on tulip poplar and clover—the two main sources of nectar at this time of the year.

He advises beekeepers—if they expect to produce any honey this year—to: Feed the bees equal parts of water and granulated sugar.

Put the mixture in a friction-top pail, which has holes or perforations in the lid.

Invert Pail

Invert the pail on top of the brood combs.

Keep it up until the bees regain their strength and the honey flow begins.

Feeding the bees sugar is an emergency measure and is badly needed now.

Rea says that Virginia's income from bee-keeping could be doubled or even tripled, simply by "doing the right thing at the right time." One colony, if properly managed, requires only about five or six hours' attention per year.

—Virginia Farm Bureau News, *June 1, 1949*

SCIENCE!

The February 1, 1946 issue of the *Highland Recorder* in Monterey reported on the USDA's research efforts: "Excellent progress in an attempt, through breeding and selection, to produce a strain of bees that is resistant to American foulbrood, one of the most fatal bee diseases."

Over in Beltsville, the research center Dr. Phillips established kept humming along. In 1948, *Virginia Farm Bureau News* announced that, under the Research and Marketing Act of 1946, twenty-two projects had been approved for the center, including efforts to discover and develop new and improved uses for apiary products.

Once the war was over, some of the Allies' chemical arsenal found its way back to the homefront. The *Rappahannock Record* began running a "Safeguarding Your Health" column from the Virginia Department of Health. On January 3, 1946, the subject was DDT:

"DDT, the war-developed insecticide, is an excellent agent against flies, clothes moths, mosquitoes, roaches, bedbugs, fleas, ants, silver fish, carpet beetles, and other insects. This substance, in its pure state, is a white and practically odorless powder It does not dissolve in water, but can be used in oil solutions, in emulsions, and as a spray. Also, it can be employed for dusting when mixed with a bland powder, such as talc," states Dr. I.C. Riggin, State Health Commissioner.

After listing numerous precautions on ventilation, handwashing, avoiding open flames, not using it to kill fleas or ticks on household pets (except in dust form), a special warning was given to beekeepers:

DDT will give satisfactory results if properly and carefully used. It must be understood, however, that its indiscriminate and negligent use can do harm not only to humans but to "good" insects. It should not be employed, for example, near hives or flowers where honey bees are at work.

Of course, compliance was purely voluntary, and DDT was outlawed in 1972. Meanwhile, the Virginia Cooperative Extension Agency was also busy spreading postwar advice. Bee Specialist Rea (misspelled as Ray in the article) did his best to be encouraging:

George H. Ray, Bee Specialist from V.P.I. will hold a meeting on honey bees, on the Rountree Dairy Farm, about two miles north of Suffolk. The idea is that all who are interested on the care and management of bees [sic]. *In no section of this country do we need more honey bees, and have less, than around here. If you never had a pound of honey from bees, their help in fertilizing your crops would be worth many times their cost and the little labor needed to manage them.*
—Suffolk News-Herald, *October 19, 1949*

UPS AND DOWNS

In 1967, the Vietnam Conflict (never officially declared a war) was underway, and the nation was rocked by protests, but it was a good year for the bees, even if the state's yield was small compared to others:

Virginia Bees Up Production

Virginia's honeycrop for 1967 was 2,266,000 pounds, according to the Virginia Crop Reporting Service. This is about 19 percent above the 1966 crop of 1,908,000. In production were 103,000 colonies for an average of 22 pounds per colony.

The early part of the season was cool and wet and this caused colonies to swarm badly. These swarms gave beekeepers a chance to fill all their empty equipment, said J.M. Amos, extension specialist, entomology....

In addition to the honey crop, beeswax totaled 45,000 pounds which is up 7 percent from 1966. The average price to beekeepers for wax was 55 cents, up 10 cents per pound.

In the United States, 223,363,000 pounds of honey were produced with California and Minnesota being the leading producers. The production average for the U.S. was 46.3 pounds per colony compared to 22 pounds in Virginia.

—Lebanon News, *February 28, 1968*

Honey fanciers were in luck in 1986, the year that the Virginia Department of Agriculture and Consumer Services published its first honey guide, available to anyone who sent it a self-addressed, stamped envelope. That first guide gave a list of twenty-two producers who offered honey and/or beekeeping supplies for sale and gave information on the types and flavors of honey to be found throughout the state, as well as information on how to store and use honey.

In 1997, state apiarist Frank Fulgham shared sobering news. In 1985, Virginia had 2,500 beekeepers and approximately 80,000 colonies of bees. Eleven years later, there were approximately 1,200 keepers minding 35,000 colonies. The stats were worse for established beekeepers with five or more hives—their 30,000 colonies in 1985 had dropped to 7,000. He also estimated that at least 90 percent of Virginia's wild honeybees had been killed by mites and viruses. With more than 90 American crops dependent on honeybees for pollination, this was bad news all around. Tracheal mites crawl into the bee's windpipe, suck its blood and reproduce there, eventually choking off the flow of oxygen. Varroa mites attach themselves to the outside of the bee and suck its blood.

Larry Kelley, then president of the Virginia State Beekeeper's Association, added that the loss of bees since the mid-1980s could be blamed on the tracheal mite—and then the Varroa mite hit the state in 1990. Treatments for the mites exist. Menthol crystals can be placed in the hives in August for tracheal mites. Varroa mites are treated with Apistan chemical strips, placed directly in the hive, in the spring before honey production and again in the fall after the last honey flow for set times. However, these measures do not eradicate the mites. They just help control the problem, according to an April 1, 1997 issue of *Farm Bureau News.*

Since at least the 1990s, farmers have been contracting with beekeepers to bring in their hives to make up for the loss in pollinators that occurred with a major wild bee die-off. But domestic hives were being stricken with mites—both Varroa and tracheal—so the situation was difficult.

In recent years, it has been quite a roller coaster. VDACS (Virginia Department of Agriculture and Consumer Services) announced that honeybee colonies for productions with five or more hives had gone up 23 percent since the start of 2016, according to a story filed for WHSV (Channel 3/Harrisonburg) by Monica Casey on August 8, 2017. Local apiary owner Mike Hott commented that the demand of backyard hobbyists for honeybees had probably gone up 80 percent in the previous three to five years.

Less than a year later, on July 24, 2018, the *Winchester Star* ran the headline "Beekeepers: Virginia's Colonies Suffer Crushing Blow, Need Help." The previous year had seen a steep decline in honeybees, and the state government and local beekeepers were back on the defense. According to VDACS, the state lost 60 percent of its bee colonies during the winter of 2017–18, the highest winter loss rate since the state began keeping that statistic in 2000. VDACS mentioned diseases, poor nutrition and pesticides as possible culprits—also Varroa and tracheal mites.

For several years, VDACS maintained a beehive distribution program to encourage new and existing beekeepers. This program worked well, as many communities loosened their regulation on beehives at the same time. A most popular program, as of this writing, it has been put on hold because of budget demands in the wake of COVID-19.

Nonetheless, VDACS offers other services to benefit beekeepers and their clients. BeeCheck (va.beecheck.org) allows beekeepers and pesticide applicators to voluntarily work together to protect apiaries through a mapping program. The Virginia Bee Law requires inspection of honeybees on combs and hives, and equipment with combs must be accompanied by a certificate of health issued by the Office of Plant Industry Services before being sold in Virginia. As far as honeybees on combs or used equipment with comb being brought in from elsewhere to be sold in Virginia, those will need to be granted an entry permit from the state apiarist.

POWER TO THE POLLINATORS

The state also keeps a list of apiaries that provide pollination services for agriculture. The contact information is provided by the apiaries themselves. This site has the links to both the registered apiaries and the form to fill out to get on the list: https://www.vdacs.virginia.gov/plant-industry-services-va-pollinator.shtml

Mount Eagle Elementary School, Alexandria, Virginia, planting pollinators, 2013. *Photo by Robert H. Pos/USFWS. (CC BY 2.0).*

Honeybees and their kin have stepped into spotlight in recent years with the creation of National Pollinator Week and Virginia Pollinator Week, held simultaneously in late June.

If honeybees aren't a possibility for you, consider creating a haven for them and others by planting pollinator-friendly plants. State apiarist Keith Tignor suggests:

> *Download the BeeSmart Pollinator Gardener app: http://www.pollinator. org/beesmartapp.htm.*
>
> *Plant a variety of flowers that bloom at different times of the year. A greater variety of plants available will attract more pollinators to a garden or landscape. Providing pollen and nectar sources throughout the year offers a food source to increase pollinator numbers and activity.*
>
> *Plant flowers in clumps rather than singly or in rows. The fragrance from the flowers can attract pollinators from a great distance. Clumping flowers in groups increases the intensity of the fragrance and a pollinator's ability to locate its origin, including those that only come out at night, such as moths and bats.*
>
> *Select plants that are known to attract pollinators in your area. Many of these will be native plants. To determine which plants are best for attracting*

pollinators in your region, go to pollinator.org/guides.htm and enter your zip code for an area-specific guide.

Choose flowers with a variety of colors. The color of a flower often alerts pollinators to good nectar and pollen sources. For example, butterflies are attracted to red, orange and yellow while hummingbirds prefer purple, red and fuchsia colors.

Choose flowers with a variety of shapes. Butterflies and honey bees need to land before feeding and usually prefer flat, open flowers. Tubular flowers help lure pollinators with long beaks and tongues, such as hummingbirds. Guidelines on the types of flowers that appeal to the different pollinators can be found at pollinator.org/Resources/Pollinator_Syndromes.pdf.

Plant non-hybrid flowers. Many hybrid flowers have had their pollen, nectar or fragrance bred out of them. Non-hybrid flowers are often more attractive to pollinators.

Do not use pesticides or herbicides when pollinators are present around a pollinator garden. Even organic pesticides can be potentially harmful to pollinators. Herbicides can actually wipe out some of the most important food plants for pollinators.

In 2020, the Virginia Department of Forestry worked with the nonprofit organization Melissae to promote bee habitat and awareness while testing the compatibility of honey production and public land management. When people think of foraging bees, they usually imagine flower meadows, gardens or fields of crops. But bees can very contentedly draw their nectar from trees, much as they did in Germany, the Slavic lands and elsewhere where forest beekeeping was common. Melissae's beekeepers have placed hives in Lesesne State Forest in Roseland (Nelson County), Virginia.

The Couvillon Lab (www.freelyflyingbees.com), part of the Department of Entomology at Virginia Tech, investigates honeybee health, recruitment and foraging. The lab connects with BeeGroup@ VT, a collaborative confederation of researchers, students, postdocs and extensionists that possess an interest in bees. Their site has information on current research projects.

ForestWander. CC BY-SA 3.0 US.

HIVES OF ACTIVITY (PLACES TO VISIT)

Virginia's Bee Cities

The Bee City USA initiative (www.beecityusa.org) encourages towns to commit to providing pollinators with healthy and sustainable habits. In 2016, Scottsville, a tiny town in both Albemarle and Fluvanna Counties, was the first town in Virginia to sign on. It is also home to the Scottsville Supply Company (www.scottsvillesupplyco.com), which has bees, beekeeping supplies and classes. Hampton, Lynchburg and Vienna have also joined the program.

Fun at the Festivals

Honeybees are often celebrated on a special day; in America, National Honeybee Day is the third Saturday in August, and festivals tend to crop up on that date. It is a time to promote beekeeping, educate the public and make others aware of environmental concerns that may affect honeybees.

Not so coincidentally in August, the Norfolk Botanical Garden hosts its Honeybee Festival with the help of the Beekeepers Guild of Southeast Virginia. Families can learn how to plant for the pollinators, taste honey samples, look inside beehives and more. (norfolkbotanicalgarden.org/events/)

Honey competitions and beekeeping demonstrations can usually be found at the State Fair of Virginia (www.statefairva.org), generally held the last week of September through the first week of October in Doswell. These and county fairs echo the agricultural fairs of earlier centuries.

If winter seems to be going on far too long, consider taking in the Richlands Winter Honey Festival, held in February. Richlands is a small town in Tazewell County, nestled in the Appalachian Mountains. Its motto, appropriate for a bee-embracing community, is "The Center of a Friendly Circle." Activities may include a pancake breakfast with honey at a local church, excursions to view wildlife and mead tasting/making. Find out more about the current year's offerings at www.facebook.com/WinterHoneyFestival/.

In June, the Virginia Beach Farmers' Market at 3640 Dam Neck Road hosts its annual Honey Festival Craft Show—a chance to enjoy honey as well as a variety of produce and crafts. Look for information at www.facebook.com/VBFarmersMarket/.

Local beekeeping associations often work in partnership with nonprofits, such as the historic sites mentioned earlier in this book, and may feature beekeeping events. Some parks, such as Sky Meadows State Park in Delaplane, have held beekeeping demonstrations in the past and may do so again.

Open Year-Round

These places have connections to bees and their history. Call or check their websites for current hours and other details. Please see the chapter on meaderies for that list. Some are open only seasonally, so check their websites for current hours.

The Bee Store, Lake Ridge, Prince William County | www.yourbeestore.com | Dropping by the Bee Store is a treat. Besides beekeeping equipment, gifts, books, mead and honey, they also have a visible hive and offer classes, both online and in person.

La Bee da Loca, Culpeper | www.labeedaloca.com | You'll find this observation hive and gift shop in the heart of downtown Culpeper. Felecia Chavez, the owner, is passionate about bee education.

Hugh Mercer Apothecary Shop Washington Heritage Museum, Fredericksburg, Virginia.
watts_photos (CC BY 2.0).

THE BOB STAPLETON & KEITH TIGNOR APIARY AT LEWIS GINTER BOTANICAL GARDEN, RICHMOND | www.lewisginter.org/apiary/ | This accessible ten-frame observation hive is in the traditional Langstroth style. The bees keep the Community Kitchen Garden well pollinated. The apiary is named for Bob Stapleton, president of the Richmond Beekeepers' Association, and Keith Tignor, the state apiarist.

COLONIAL WILLIAMSBURG: APOTHECARY SHOP AND GARDENS | www. colonialwilliamsburg.org/locations/apothecary/ | Drop by the apothecary and its gardens as part of your tour of Colonial Williamsburg.

HUGH MERCER APOTHECARY SHOP, FREDERICKSBURG | www. washingtonheritagemuseums.org | A longtime favorite of local visitors, the re-created apothecary shop of an eighteenth-century physician and Revolutionary War general gives a lively introduction to the art of colonial medicine.

JAMESTOWN REDISCOVERY: HISTORIC JAMESTOWN | Historicjamestowne.org | Tour the living history recreation of the earliest permanent English colony. You will likely spy a skep or two.

MEADERIES | Virginia has numerous meaderies spread throughout the state. See the chapter "Sweet Spirits at Meaderies" and "Virginia's Mead Path" (page 106) for listings.

RIPPON LODGE HISTORIC SITE, WOODBRIDGE, PRINCE WILLIAM COUNTY | www.pwcgov.org/government/dept/park/hp/Pages/Rippon-Lodge.aspx | Rippon Lodge, a colonial-era house once home to the Blackburn family, now (or likely again) keeps bees, although they are not part of the regular tour. Check their calendar for special "Bee Encounter" events.

ROCKWOOD NATURE CENTER, CHESTERFIELD COUNTY | www.chesterfield. gov/Facilities/Facility/Details/Rockwood-Nature-Center-71 | Bring lunch, and after you eat, visit the Rockwood Nature Center, where you can experience live snake, turtle, and honeybee exhibits.

Spikenard Farm Honeybee Sanctuary, Floyd County | www.
Spikenardfarm.org | The forty-one-acre sanctuary is home to over thirty
honeybee hives. They promote sustainable beekeeping through education
and experience-based research.

The Virginia Zoo: The Observation Hive at ZooFarm, Norfolk | www.
virginiazoo.org | Visitors can see the bees at stages of development and
may be able to spot the queen, as she is wearing a bright dot. The hive is
helped by the Norfolk Beekeepers.

HONEY-SWEET TREATS
TO DRINK AND EAT

These recipes harken to past times. Before there was pizza pie with tomato sauce, there was focaccia. The name comes from the Latin *panis focacius*, meaning, "hearth bread." Lovely with a simple soup or dipped in herbed olive oil, the roasted red bell pepper is a New World addition.

Honey Garlic Focaccia with Rosemary and Roasted Peppers
Yield: Makes 6 focaccia

Ingredients
2½ to 3 cups all-purpose flour
1 package fast-rising yeast
1 teaspoon salt
¾ cup water
¼ cup plus 1 tablespoon honey
1 tablespoon olive oil
1 tablespoon finely chopped garlic
6 tablespoons chopped roasted red bell pepper, drained
2 teaspoons chopped fresh rosemary
Cornmeal

Directions
In large bowl, combine 2 cups flour, undissolved yeast and salt. Heat water, ¼ cup honey and oil until very warm (120° to 130°F); stir

into dry ingredients. Stir in garlic and enough remaining flour to make soft dough. Knead on lightly floured surface until smooth and elastic, about 6 to 8 minutes. Cover; let rest 10 minutes.

Divide dough into 6 equal pieces. Roll each into a 4-by-5-inch oval.

Sprinkle 2 large baking sheets with cornmeal. Place dough pieces on sheets. Sprinkle each piece with 1 tablespoon roasted pepper and ¼ teaspoon rosemary. Cover; let rise in warm, draft-free place until doubled in size, about 30 to 45 minutes. Bake at 400°F for 12 to 15 minutes or until done.

Warm remaining honey; drizzle on top of focaccias. Remove from sheets; cool on wire rack.

BREAD MACHINE VARIATION (all-size machines): Measure 2⅔ cups flour, yeast, salt, water, ¼ cup honey, oil and garlic into bread machine pan as suggested by manufacturer. Process on dough/ manual cycle. When complete, remove dough to floured surface; knead in additional flour if necessary to make dough easy to handle. Roll out dough and proceed as directed. (National Honey Board, www.honey.com)

Delicious Corn Muffins

Corn, as in maize, was grown by American Indian tribes and adopted by the settlers. They used it for everything from corn fritters to corn whiskey. Corn muffins were a particular favorite. This wartime recipe saved the staple goods, such as wheat flour and sugar, that were needed at the front. There are no directions for baking it, but the usual temperature for muffins is 400 degrees until testing done, about 12 minutes:

Here's an old-fashioned recipe for corn muffins that has recently been revived and used with unusual success in several of the larger New York hotels: To make three and a half dozen muffins take one quart milk, six ounces butter substitute, twelve ounces of light syrup or honey, four eggs, pinch of salt, two ounces baking powder, one and a half pounds cornmeal and one and a half pounds rye flour. The butter and syrup should be thoroughly mixed; then add the eggs gradually. Pour in the milk and add the rye flour mixed with cornmeal and baking powder. From the Clinch Valley News, *February 1, 1918.*

Honey Gingerbread Cookies

A childhood favorite rediscovers its honeyed past—ginger cookies were (and are) popular in Britain and Germany, but the American versions have long featured molasses. This makes a cookie with a delicate and delicious flavor.

Ingredients
1½ cups honey
¾ cup butter or margarine, softened
1 egg
5 cups all-purpose flour
2 teaspoons baking powder
1 tablespoon ground ginger
1 tablespoon ground cinnamon
1 teaspoon ground cloves

Directions
In large bowl, cream honey and butter until light and fluffy. Beat in egg. Add flour, baking powder, ginger, cinnamon and cloves; mix until combined. Wrap dough in plastic wrap and refrigerate for at least 2 hours. When dough is chilled, divide in half; return one half to refrigerator.

Dust work surface and dough with flour. Roll out dough to ¼-inch thick. Cut into desired shapes using cookie cutters; transfer to well-greased baking sheet. Bake at 350°F for 10 to 12 minutes. Remove cookies from sheet and cool on wire rack. Repeat with remaining dough. (National Honey Board, www.honey.com)

Honey Wheat Pretzel Rolls

A nod to the German settlers of the Shenandoah Valley
Yield: Makes 16 rolls

Ingredients
1⅓ cups whole milk, warm (about 110° F)
1 cup water, warm (about 110° F)
2¼ teaspoons yeast
3 tablespoons honey
2 tablespoons butter, melted
2½ cups all-purpose flour
2½ cups whole wheat flour
1½ teaspoons kosher salt
Egg wash or milk for brushing
Sesame seeds (optional)
Pretzel salt or coarse sea salt, for sprinkling (optional)

Directions

Combine milk, water, yeast and honey in the bowl of a stand mixer. Let sit 5 to 10 minutes until mixture is foamy. Add butter and set aside.

Mix flours and salt in a big bowl. Slowly add the flour mixture into the milk-yeast mixture with mixer running on low (hook attachment) until the dough pulls away from the bottom of the bowl and a dough forms. Knead dough on low speed for 3–5 minutes until smooth and pliable.

Place the dough in a lightly greased bowl. Cover and let rise for 2 hours at room temperature. Dust your work surface with a little flour and turn the risen dough out on top. Divide the dough into 16 pieces. To shape into rolls, roll the dough against the counter until round. Place the balls on a lightly greased baking sheet, cover, and let rest for 15 minutes.

Preheat oven to 425°F. Brush each roll generously with whole milk or egg wash, then sprinkle with sesame seeds and pretzel salt, if desired. Bake 20 minutes until rolls are golden brown and baked through. Remove them from the oven and serve. (National Honey Board, www.honey.com)

Honey Mint Julep

A favorite at race meets or when entertaining on any warm day.

Ingredients
2 tablespoons boiling water (easiest to pour from a kettle)
8 mint leaves
1½ tablespoons honey
2 ounces bourbon, per serving
Crushed ice
Mint sprigs, for garnish

Directions
Pour boiling water from a kettle or pot into a small bowl. Add mint leaves; stir until wilted. Add honey; stir until dissolved. Let mixture stand until cool; strain and discard mint.

Combine 2 oz. bourbon with honey mint syrup. Pour bourbon mixture over crushed ice in a frosted tumbler or tall glass. Garnish with mint sprigs. (National Honey Board, www.honey.com)

Peach and Honey, New York Style

Eventually, peach and honey found its way to the North, possibly offered to sojourning southerners at race meets. The Bartender's Guide: How to Mix Drinks by Jerry Thomas (1862) gives this simple recipe, truly a shortcut:

1 table-spoon honey
1 wine-glass peach brandy

(Use small bar glass.) Stir with a spoon.

Strawberry Rose Shrub Syrup

Shrubs, an alternative to alcoholic beverages, were popular with the temperance crowd and are making a comeback today. This version combines ripe strawberries with rosewater—available at Middle Eastern markets or online if you don't have the summer and the blossoms to make your own. Equal parts honey and cider vinegar create a beverage that is sweet and sharp.

Yield: Makes 4 cups

Ingredients
4 cups strawberries, hulled and cut in half
2 cups honey
1 cup sugar
2 cups cider vinegar
2 tablespoons edible lavender
4 1-inch strips lemon zest
$\frac{1}{4}$ cup rose water

Directions
Combine the strawberries, honey, sugar, vinegar, lavender and lemon zest in a nonreactive saucepan and gently mash the strawberries a bit with the back of a wooden spoon. Bring mixture to a boil for 2 minutes and then lower to a simmer for another 10 minutes, remove from heat and let the fruit steep for an hour.

Strain the mixture with a sieve and stir in the rose water. Decant into an airtight jar or bottle and seal. Refrigerate and enjoy with seltzer or as a base for cocktails for up to a week.

Tip: Nonreactive cookware includes ones that are glass, stainless steel, nonstick or enamel. Using reactive cookware such as copper, aluminum and cast iron with acidic ingredients like vinegar can create a metallic taste in the finished dish. (National Honey Board. www.honey.com)

HONEY AND ITS USES IN THE HOME

Newspapers often reprinted helpful information from the government. In this case, the information for the Farmers' Bulletin may have come from Dr. Phillips' Bee Culture Lab. The National Honey Board, which supplied many of the more modern recipes in this section, is also an offshoot of the USDA.

World News, *April 14, 1915*
Washington, D.C. April 14.

Various ways in which the housewife can use honey to advantage are suggested in a new publication of the United States Department of Agriculture, Farmers' Bulletin 653, "Honey and Its Uses in the Home." In this country honey has hitherto not been in as common use as in Europe, especially in cookery. It is, however, a comparatively simple matter to substitute it in many recipes for common sugar or for molasses, and when this is done the resulting flavor is often both novel and agreeable.

One of the great advantages in the use of honey is that cakes made with it will keep much longer than those made with sugar. A honey cake, made with butter, for instance, will keep its quality until the butter grows rancid, and one made without butter will keep fresh for months. For this reason, honey is especially useful in recipes that call for no butter. Icing made with honey has the same advantage, and some icing made in the experimental laboratory of the department of agriculture was found at the end of ten months to be as soft and in as good condition as it was first made.

The experiments conducted by the department indicate that many of the instructions in the old cookbooks for the preparation of honey are unnecessarily elaborate. For example, it used to be taught that honey had to be brought to the boiling point and then skimmed and cooled. Since honey is extremely likely to boil over, this process requires great care. Experiments showed, however, that it appears to be quite unnecessary, and it is probable that the notion arose at a time when ordinary commercial honey contained more impurities than at present. Similarly, the older recipes say that the dough should be kept at least one day before the soda is added. No evidence to support this theory was found by the investigators. On the other hand, however, they did discover that dough containing honey can be more easily kneaded if allowed to stand for several days. Again, the use of "potash" is recommended in most of the recipes in foreign cookbooks as a means of raising the dough. The properties of potash are quite similar to ordinary baking soda, and there seems no reason why the latter should not do just as well. Baking soda is a common kitchen commodity in America, and potassium bicarbonate—the potash of the cookery book—is almost unknown for household purposes. As a matter of fact, a little experience will enable any competent cook to substitute honey successfully for sugar in bread, cake, preserved fruits, sauces, and candies. It is safe to estimate that a cupful of honey will sweeten a dish about as much as a cupful of sugar but since honey contains water in addition, there is less need for milk or other liquids. For practical purposes, it is accurate enough to consider that for each cupful of honey, a quarter of a cupful is added to the recipe. If these facts are kept in mind, special honey recipes are unnecessary.

Honey is marketed in two forms, known respectively as comb honey and extracted honey, the former being used much like jam or marmalade, and the latter either in that way or for cooking. In the past, there has been some prejudice against extracted honey—or honey removed from the comb—because it was believed that this was frequently adulterated. However prevalent this practice may have been in the past, recent legislation and the efforts of honey producers themselves have made it dangerous and unprofitable. There is now, it is believed, little adulterated extracted honey on the market. Comb honey is practically certain to be the pure product of the hive because it can only be adulterated by processes which cost more than they save. When sold at retail there is now comparatively little difference in the cost of comb and extracted honey, but the latter can be purchased at wholesale very much cheaper. The reason for this is that the producer of comb honey makes a product which is practically ready to be delivered to the consumer. Moreover, it costs the bee-keeper less to produce extracted honey while the wholesaler who purchases extracted honey has several processes to go through with before he can sell it at retail. If the housewife is willing to do these herself, she can effect a considerable saving.

The simplest and, perhaps, most popular way of using honey is to serve it like jam or sirup, with bread, pancakes, etc. When used in this way an ounce of honey may be regarded as the equivalent of an ounce of jam. When intended for sirup, it is sometimes diluted with hot water, not only to make it less sweet, but also easier to pour. The housewife will also find some form of tart fruit served with honey, cottage cheese, and bread and butter, an attractive combination, and an economical substitute for the much-prized and very expensive Bar-le-Duck currants which are themselves often cooked in honey and served with cream cheese and crackers. The following are typical of an almost endless number of honey recipes:

Honey and Nut Bran Muffins

1 cup flour
From ¼ to ½ teaspoon soda
¼ teaspoon salt
2 cups bran
½ cup honey
1 tablespoon melted butter
1½ cups milk
¾ cup finely chopped English walnuts.

Sift together the flour, soda and salt, and mix them with the bran. Add the other ingredients, and bake for 25 or 20 minutes in a hot oven (400–425 degrees) in gem tins (similar to muffin tins). This will make about 20 muffins. From the *World News*, April 14, 1915

Scripture Cake

Here's a recipe written in code, as each Bible verse references an ingredient, and most versions do not include a cipher. This cake was—and is—a favorite in the church fellowship hall for Sunday morning coffee or for after–Bible study treats, King Solomon's advice notwithstanding.

4½ cups I Kings 4:22 (flour)
1½ cups Judges 5:25 (butter, level cup)
2 cups Jeremiah 6:20 (sugar)
2 cups I Samuel 30:12 (raisins)
2 cups Nahum 3:12 (figs)
1 cup Numbers 17:8 (almonds)
2 tablespoons I Samuel 14:25 (honey)
Season to taste with II Chronicles 9:9 (spices)
6 Jeremiah 17:11 (eggs)
A pinch of Leviticus 2:13 (salt)
1½ cups Judges 4:19 (milk, level cup)
2 teaspoons Amos 4:5 (baking powder)

Follow Solomon's prescription for making a good boy by Proverbs 23:14: "Thou shalt beat him with the rod," and the cake should be extra good, suitable for church suppers. From the *Norfolk Post*, September 19, 1921

Editor's modern summary: First, cream butter and sugar. Then, add honey, milk and eggs—one at a time. Add spices (your choice), baking powder, salt and flour. Lightly dredge raisins, chopped almonds and chopped figs in flour, then fold into batter. Put batter in a well-greased and floured full-size Bundt pan or tube cake pan. Bake at 325 degrees for approximately 1 hour, or until cake tests done. Lightly separate cake from sides of pan with a table knife. Let cool in pan 10 minutes, then invert onto cake plate. Dust with powdered sugar or use a flavored drizzle.

SO, YOU WANT TO BE A BEEKEEPER...

Perhaps you are considering becoming a beekeeper. First, see if your local ordinances allow it. For some decades, it was difficult for people who did not live in the countryside to keep bees, but the rise in interest, particularly after the Colony Collapse Disorder events, has encouraged many local governments to loosen their restrictions to help the bees.

The next logical step is to check in with your regional beekeeping group. You can find them through the state beekeeper's association. If you live in Virginia, that will be the Virginia State Beekeepers' Association: www.virginiabeekeepers.org. Look under INFORMATION & RESOURCES TO FIND A LOCAL CLUB. Clubs hold meetings several times a year. They are very much on top of the latest news of interest to beekeepers and are a great source of knowledge for new beekeepers. Their knowledge is local, which is crucial since hive conditions can be local, and what is working for the tidewater area may not work in the cooler mountain temperatures. Experienced beekeepers may participate in Swarm Removal Hotlines, where the public can let the beekeepers know where the stray swarms are resting so they can gather them and rehome them.

Many clubs offer classes on beekeeping for their members and serve as mentors for new beekeepers. The next step would be to take an introductory class in beekeeping to see if it is something you want to commit to. Besides local clubs, the Virginia Cooperative Extension Agency may offer classes in your county or a nearby one. Contact a local office to ask about classes or inquire about their Master Beekeeper program: https://ext.vt.edu/offices.html

"Removing the Queen Cage from the New Hive." Beekeeping at Sky Meadows. *vastateparksstaff.*
Creative Commons 2.0 license.

Sky Meadows Meet the Beekeepers Weekend. *vastateparksstaff. Creative Commons 2.0 license.*

SPECIAL OPPORTUNITIES

Availability of funding for the state's BEEHIVE DISTRIBUTION PROGRAM to individuals waxes and wanes, but it is part of the Virginia Code, so it is worth investigating to see if it is active: https://www.vdacs.virginia.gov/plant-industry-services-beehive-distribution-program.shtml

Perhaps you are thinking beyond maintaining a few beehives. The Cooperative Extension has a NEW AND BEGINNING FARMER & RANCHER PROGRAM that provides training for minorities, U.S. military veterans and the socially disadvantaged. They provide education, outreach, hands-on experiential learning, training, and technical assistance as well as farmer-mentor support: https://www.ext.vsu.edu/sdvbfr-program

As mentioned earlier, Dr. Phillips was keen on the idea of promoting beekeeping for veterans, and this is something which has been repeated time after time. HIVES FOR HEROES is a national military veteran nonprofit organization focusing on honeybee conservation, suicide prevention and a healthy transition from service. They provide purpose, connections and healthy relationships fostering a lifelong hobby in beekeeping: https://www.hivesforheroes.com/. The online guide GOVERNMENT RESOURCES FOR FARMER

Thomas and Anita Roberson (both U.S. Army veterans) operate the Roberson Farm Tour in Fredericksburg, Virginia. *Photo by Preston Keres/USDA; public domain.*

Thomas Roberson tending the hives. *Photo by Preston Keres/USDA; public domain.*

VETERANS can help those navigating USDA and other federal government resource programs: https://farmvetco.org/wp-content/uploads/2020/03/Government-Resources-Guide-for-Farmer-Veterans-sized-down.pdf

If you elect to sell your products or want to know where to go to buy, VDACS has a list of farmers' markets by region: https://www.vdacs.virginia.gov/vagrown/frmsmkt-resources.shtml. The Virginia's Finest program, which helps promote high-quality foods produced in the state, does include honey and honey products: https://www.vdacs.virginia.gov/vafinest.com/index.shtml

STATE REGULATIONS

Aside from your local ordinances, there are state regulations, which mainly affect commercial operations, but you should be aware that there are requirements for transporting bees and used equipment into Virginia. This is perfectly understandable considering what a lot of damage can be caused by introducing unhealthy bees into a hive. You can read about VIRGINIA'S BEE LAWS here: http://law.lis.virginia.gov/vacode/title3.2/chapter44/

Three of the eight beehives of Brookview Farm in Manakin-Sabot, Virginia, that produce honey for Fall Line Farms, a local food cooperative in the Richmond area, 2011. *USDA photos by Lance Cheung; public domain.*

Those interested in producing honey for sale are advised to check with the Office of the State Apiarist: VABees@vdacs.virginia.gov. The Food Safety Program handbook (pp. 38-39, 53, 97) will also be of interest: http://www.vdacs.virginia.gov/pdf/va-food-handbook.pdf. Always check with the VDACS for the most current regulations.

OTHER WAYS TO HELP THE BEES

If you decide keeping bees isn't for you, you can still help the pollinators by planting a pollinator-friendly garden. VIRGINIA NATIVES, a website hosted by the Virginia Department of Environmental Quality, has suggestions and regional guides: https://www.plantvirginianatives.org/.

Also, buying local bee products—at farmers markets, farm markets, specialty shops or from the beekeepers themselves—is a wonderful way to support beekeepers and their bees. There are many apiaries in the state. VDAC's Virginia Grown directory lists honey and honey product vendors: http://vagrown.va-vdacs.com/Default.aspx?category=HONEY.

ACKNOWLEDGEMENTS

With thanks…

Any project of this nature requires a good deal of assistance, particularly in a time of lockdown. The author would like to thank Dawn Bonner, manager of visual resources, George Washington's Mount Vernon & Mount Vernon Ladies' Association; the Copeland family, Misty Mountain Meadworks; Samantha Duncan, Central Rappahannock Regional Library; Lauren Fleming, registrar/collections manager, Museum of the Shenandoah Valley; Matthew Guillen, reference coordinator, Virginia Museum of History & Culture; Judy Hynson, director of research and library collections for Stratford Hall Plantation; John Klapperich, the Bee Store; Michael Kimball, Consociate Media; Glenn Lavender, founder/ owner of Silver Hand Meadery; Tina Miller, Public Services and Outreach

Modern-day beekeeper examining a frame from a hive. *Courtesy of the Mount Vernon Ladies' Association.*

Division, Library of Virginia; Gardiner Mulford, owner of Gardiner's Farm and Maidstone Meadery; Holt Saulsgiver, office and grounds manager, Tuckahoe; and Gina Woodward, delivery service coordinator, Swem Library, College of William & Mary.

With a special thanks for those who saw it through from start to finish: Kate Jenkins, the wise and ever-patient editor for The History Press and Arcadia Publishing, and my husband, Steve Johnson, who braved bees, sampled mead, read proof on the manuscript and served as resident polymath.

BIBLIOGRAPHY

Aesop. "The Bear & the Bees." In *The Aesop for Children: with Pictures by Milo Winter*, published by Rand, McNally & Co in 1919. An interactive storybook at the Library of Congress. http://read.gov/aesop/001.html.

Alston, Frank. *Skeps: Their History, Making and Use*. Scout Bottom Farm, West Yorkshire: Northern Bee Books, 1987.

American Bee Journal. "Convention Proceedings of the North American Bee-Keepers' Association." October 29, 1896, 1. https://archive.org/stream/americanbeejourn3696hami/#page/689/mode/1up.

Angotti, Laura D. *Wellcome Mead: 105 Mead Recipes from 17th and 18th Century English Receipt Manuscripts at the Wellcome Library*. Arlington, MA: Mt. Gilboa Miscellany, 2019.

Aristotle's History of Animals in Ten Books. Book the Fifth, Chapters XVIII & XIX. Translated by Richard Cresswell. London: George Bell & Sons, York Street, Covent Garden, 1887. https://www.gutenberg.org/files/59058/59058-h/59058-h.htm

Bacon, A.M., and E.C. Parsons. "Folk-Lore from Elizabeth City County, Virginia." *Journal of American Folklore* 35, no. 137 (1922): 274–75.

Barton, B. "Some Account of the Poisonous and Injurious Honey of North America." *Transactions of the American Philosophical Society* 5 (1802): 51–70. https://www.jstor.org/stable/i241957.

Baumstark, Heidi. "Fertile Ground for Learning—Former School Site Now Home of Manassas Museum." *Manassas Observer*, January 23, 2015.

Beverley, Robert. *The History and Present State of Virginia, In Four Parts*. London: Printed for R. Parker, 1705. https://docsouth.unc.edu/southlit/beverley/beverley.html

Blow, William Nivison. *Tower Hill: Before the Rebellion: A History of the Small Virginia Plantation Before the Civil War*. Williamsburg: Earl Gregg Swem Library, Special Collections, 1991. https://digitalarchive.wm.edu/bitstream/handle/10288/13353/towerhill.pdf.

Brendle, Reverend Thomas R., and C.W. Unger. "Folk Medicine of the Pennsylvania Germans." In *The Pennsylvania German Society*. Norristown, PA: Norristown Herald Inc., 1935. https://archive.org/stream/pennsylvaniagerm06penn/pennsylvaniagerm06penn_djvu.txt

Calo, Mary Ann. "Winslow Homer's Visits to Virginia during Reconstruction." *American Art Journal* 12, no. 1 (Winter 1980): 4–27.

Caron, Dewey M. "Where It All Began." *Journal of the Eastern Apicultural Society of North America* 45, no. 1 (2018): 18–19. https://www.easternapiculture.org/images/journal/Spring_2018.pdf

Clarke, Peyton Neale. *Old King William Homes and Families: An Account of Some of the Old Homesteads and Families of King William County, Virginia*. Louisville, KY: J.P. Morton and Co., 1897. http://genealogytrails.com/vir/kingwilliam/county_history.html.

Colonial Williamsburg Foundation. "Bees in the Colonies." http://podcasts.history.org/100509/BeesintheColonies.cfm.

Columella, Lucius Junius. *Of Husbandry: In Twelve Books: and His Book Concerning Trees*. London: A. Millar, 1745. https://www.google.com/books/edition/L_Junius_Moderatus_Columella_Of_Husbandr/qcNbAAAAMAAJ?hl=en.

Cooper, James Fenimore. *The Oak Openings: Or The Bee-Hunter*. London: G. Routledge, 1856. https://www.google.com/books/edition/_/PWwJAAAAQAAJ?hl=en&sa=X&ved=2ahUKEwi_i6Gt4LDvAhWDuVkKHfhaBGEQ7_IDMBN6BAgTEAI.

Cowen, David L. "The Folk Medicine of the Pennsylvania Dutch." *Pharmacy in History* 55, no. 2/3 (2013): 88–95.

Crane, Eva. *The World History of Beekeeping and Honey Hunting*. New York: Routledge, 1999.

Dixon, Luke. *Keeping Bees in Towns and Cities*. Portland, OR: Timber Press, 2012.

Founders Online. "Solomon Henkel to Thomas Jefferson, 5 July 1817." https://founders.archives.gov/documents/Jefferson/03-11-02-0422.

George Washington's Mount Vernon. "George Washington: Bee Keeper." https://www.mountvernon.org/blog/2018/07/george-washington-bee-keeper.

Gill, Harold B., Jr. "Dr. De Sequeyra's 'Diseases of Virginia.'" *Virginia Magazine of History and Biography*, July 1978.

Greengrass, M., M. Leslie and M. Hannon. *The Hartlib Papers*. Sheffield, UK: Digital Humanities Institute, University of Sheffield, 2013. https://www.dhi.ac.uk/hartlib.

Grendon, Felix. "The Anglo-Saxon Charms." *Journal of American Folklore* 22 (1909): 105–237.

Hand, W. "Anglo-American Folk Belief and Custom: The Old World's Legacy to the New." *Journal of the Folklore Institute* 7, no. 2/3 (1970): 136–55.

Harris, Roger Deane. *The Story of the Bloods: Including an Account of the Early Generations of the Family in America*. Boston: C.K. Hall and Co., 1960. https://archive.org/stream/storyofbloodsinc00unse/storyofbloodsinc00unse_djvu.txt.

Hartlib, Samuel. *The Reformed Common-Wealth of Bees*. London: Printed for Giles Calvert at the Black-Spread-Eagle at the West-end of Pauls, 1655. https://quod.lib.umich.edu/e/eebo/A45759.0001.001?view=toc.

Herndon, G. "Elliott L. Story: A Small Farmer's Struggle for Economic Survival in Antebellum Virginia." *Agricultural History* 56, no. 3 (July 1982): 516–27.

JSTOR. Numerous academic articles were sourced through this database. It may be available through your local public or academic library. https://www.jstor.org.

Loomis, C. "Some Lore of Yankee Genius, 1831–1863." *Western Folklore* 6, no. 4 (1947): 341–50.

Mangum Wyatt A. "An Early History of the Honey Extractor in America." *American Bee Journal*. September 1, 2016. https://americanbeejournal.com/early-history-honey-extractor-america/.

McCulloch-Williams, Martha. *Dishes & Beverages of the Old South*. New York: McBride, Nast & Company, 1913. https://n2t.net/ark:/85335/m5538j.

Meacham, Sarah Hand. "'They Will Be Adjudged by Their Drink, What Kinde of Housewives They Are': Gender, Technology, and Household Cidering in England and the Chesapeake, 1690 to 1760." *Virginia Magazine of History and Biography*, 2003.

Mid-Atlantic Apiculture Research and Extension Consortium. "Selecting the Right Type of Bee." https://canr.udel.edu/maarec/selecting-the-right-type-of-bee/.

Miner, T.B. *The American Bee Keeper's Manual*. New York: C.M. Saxton, 1851. https://www.google.com/books/edition/The_American_Bee_Keeper_s_Manual/OYo5AQAAMAAJ?hl=en.

Morrison, A.J. "Note on the Organization of Virginia Agriculture." *William and Mary Quarterly* 26, no. 3 (1918): 169–73.

Morse, Roger. *Making Mead (Honey Wine): History, Recipes, Methods and Equipment*. Kalamazoo, MI: Wicwas Press, 1980.

Ordal, Hailey. "This Land of Milk and Honey: How the Honey Bee Shaped America." Foundation for the Preservation of Honey Bees, Inc. https://preservationofhoneybees.org/essays/2014-4h-essays/item/6-hailey-ordal

Penman, Leigh T.I. "Omnium Exposita Rapinæ: The Afterlives of the Papers of Samuel Hartlib." In *Book History*, vol. 19, 1–65. Baltimore: Johns Hopkins University Press, 2016.

Prowell, George Reeser. *History of the Eighty-Seventh Regiment, Pennsylvania Volunteers*. York, PA: Press of the York Daily, 1901. https://archive.org/details/historyofeightys00prow_0.

Pryor, Elizabeth. *Honey, Maple Sugar and Other Farm Produced Sweeteners in the Colonial Chesapeake*. The National Colonial Farm Research Report No. 19. Accokeek, MD: Accokeek Foundation Inc., 1983.

Rappahannock Record. "Legends Surround the Old, Huge Ghost Tree." February 17, 1994.

Records of the Virginia Company of London. "Letter of December 5, 1621." Virtual Jamestown. http://www.virtualjamestown.org/exist/cocoon/jamestown/virgco/b002245360.

Reid, John. *The Scot's Gard'ner, Together with the Gard'ners Kalendar*. David Lindsay and His Partners, Edinburg, at the Foot of Heriot's Bridge, 1683. (1907 edition) https://electricscotland.com/books/pdf/The%20Scots%20Gardner.pdf.

"Robbing a Wild-Bee Hive." *Harper's Weekly*, November 3, 1883.

Root, A.I., and E.R. Root. *The ABC and XYZ of Bee Culture*. Medina, OH: A.I. Root Company, 1921. https://www.biodiversitylibrary.org/item/182116#page/13/mode/1up.

Schlebecker, John T. "Farmers in the Lower Shenandoah Valley, 1850." *Virginia Magazine of History and Biography*, October 1971.

Smith, Elmer L. Madison College. "Christmas Customs." *Recorder* 90, no. 51 (1967): 2.

Thomas, Jerry. *The Bartender's Guide: How to Mix Drinks*. New York: Dick & Fitzgerald, 1862.

Thomas Jefferson Encyclopedia. "Bees and Honey." https://www.monticello.org/site/research-and-collections/bees-and-honey.

Thompson, Mary. "George Washington and Bees." https://washingtonpapers.org/george-washington-and-bees.

Turner, Charles. W. "Virginia State Agricultural Societies, 1811–1860." *Agricultural History* 38, no. 3 (July 1964): 167–77.

Tusser, Thomas. *Five Hundred Pointes of Good Husbandrie.* Imprinted at London, by Henrie Denham, dwelling in Paternoster Row, at the signe of the Starre, 1580. https://www.gutenberg.org/files/51764/51764-h/51764-h.htm.

Virgil. *The Georgics, Book IV.* http://classics.mit.edu/Virgil/georgics.4.iv.html.

Virginia Chronicle Newspaper Archive. Library of Virginia. (Miscellaneous Virginia newspaper articles were sourced from this.) https://virginiachronicle.com.

Walker, P., & Crane, E. "The History of Beekeeping in English Gardens." *Garden History*, 28 no. 2 (2000): 231-261.

Warner, Deborah Jean. *Sweet Stuff: An American History of Sweeteners, from Sugar to Sucralose.* Washington, D.C.: Smithsonian Institution Scholarly Press, 2011.

Wertenbaker, Thomas J. *The Planters of Colonial Virginia.* New York: Russell & Russell, 1959. http://library.beau.org/gutenberg/3/2/5/0/32507/32507-h/32507-h.htm.

Wildman, Thomas. *A Treatise on the Management of Bees.* 1768. https://www.google.com/books/edition/A_Treatise_on_the_Management_of_Bees/CCZAAAAAcAAJ?hl=en.

Wilson, C. "Notes on Folk-Medicine." *Journal of American Folklore* 21, no. 80 (1908): 68–73.

Worsham, John H. *One of Jackson's Foot Cavalry: His Experience and What He Saw During the War 1861–1865.* New York: Neale Publishing Company, 1912. https://docsouth.unc.edu/fpn/worsham/worsham.html.

Youman, A.E. *A Dictionary of Every-Day Wants Containing Twenty Thousand Receipts in Nearly Every Department of Human Effort.* St. Louis, MO: Continental Publishing Company, 1872. https://archive.org/details/dictionaryofever00youmiala.

INDEX

ABOUT THE AUTHOR

Virginia Johnson is the web content librarian at Central Rappahannock Regional Library. She has a Bachelor of Arts degree in anthropology from the College of William & Mary and earned her Master of Library Science degree from The University of Maryland at College Park. She lives in historic Fredericksburg with her husband, Steve, and son, Benedict. Her previous award-winning books, *Virginia Horse Racing: Triumphs of the Turf* and *Virginia by Stagecoach*, are also available from The History Press/Arcadia Publishing.

Visit us at
www.historypress.com